Venice and Amsterdam

A study of seventeenth-century élites

In the same series

KNIGHTS AND SAMURAI
Feudalism in Northern France and Japan
by Archibald Lewis

Venice and Amsterdam

A study of seventeenth-century élites

PETER BURKE

TEMPLE SMITH · LONDON

First published in Great Britain 1974
by Maurice Temple Smith Ltd
37 Great Russell Street, London WC1
© PETER BURKE 1974
ISBN 0 8511 7052 8
Printed in Great Britain by
Lowe & Brydone (Printers) Ltd, Thetford, Norfolk

ISBN # 06-136157-7

Contents

Illustrations

(between pages 112 and 113)

For Squirrel

A merchant is accustomed to employ his money chiefly in profitable projects; whereas a mere country gentleman is accustomed to employ it chiefly in expense. The one often sees his money go from him and return to him again with a profit: the other, when he parts with it, very seldom expects to see any more of it. Those different habits naturally affect their temper and disposition in every sort of business. A merchant is commonly a bold; a country gentleman, a timid undertaker. . . . The habits, beside, of order, economy and attention, to which mercantile business naturally forms a merchant, render him much fitter to execute, with profit and success, any project of improvement.

Adam Smith, *The Wealth of Nations*, Book III, Chapter 4

The Study of Élites

This book is an essay in comparative social history. It is only in the last few years, more particularly in France, the USA and Great Britain, that social history has become a serious independent discipline. It is becoming as rigorous in its methods as economic history, after a long period in which it was the preserve of amateurs and antiquarians, who collected (as Croker wrote, cruelly but correctly, of Macaulay's famous third chapter) no more than an 'old curiosity shop' of miscellaneous information. The fault was partly in the negative conception of social history current until quite recently, a conception expressed in George Macaulay Trevelyan's notorious definition of it as 'history with the politics left out'.[1] The new social history might be defined more positively as the study of social change in specific communities, where 'social change' means change in the social structure, the groups which make up society. The new social historians attempt to combine the attention to detail and the interest in change over time characteristic of the traditional historian with the social scientist's interest in problems, and so in comparisons. They tend to focus on the history of particular social groups in specific regions over a generation, a century or even longer. Examples that spring to mind are E. P. Thompson on the English working class in the early nineteenth century; Lawrence Stone on the English peerage, 1558-1641; Elinor Barber on the bourgeoisie in eighteenth-century France; Marc Raeff on the nobility of eighteenth-century Russia; Hans Rosenberg on aristocrats and bureaucrats in Prussia; and Emmanuel Le Roy Ladurie on the peasants of Languedoc in the sixteenth and seventeenth centuries.

The historian of aristocracies, at least, can learn something from the sociological study of 'élites', defined throughout this book as groups high on three criteria; status, power and wealth. The dominant figure in the sociological study of élites is, of course, Vilfredo Pareto, author of the *Treatise on General Sociology* (1916). Pareto raided history for his own purposes; historians might well make use of him for theirs. His model of society was one of a 'system' of parts or particles interacting to produce 'social equilibrium'. The social historian may find it useful (without necessarily committing himself to a grand general theory) to look at the interaction of economic, political and cultural factors in the life of a social group. Pareto argued that an important mechanism of social equilibrium was what he called the 'circulation of élites'. He distinguished types of élite such as 'lions' (military) and 'foxes' (political); or 'rentiers' and 'speculators' (or perhaps 'entrepreneurs'). Rentiers are essentially men on fixed incomes, while entrepreneurs pursue profit. However, true to his emphasis on the impact of one part of the social system on another, Pareto used these terms to refer not only to the economic basis of the two élites but to their intellectual and psychological make-up. Entrepreneurs are active, imaginative, interested in innovation, 'speculators' in the philosophical as well as in the economic sense of the term. Rentiers are passive, unimaginative, conservative. The distinction is not unlike Adam Smith's distinction between the 'merchant' and the 'gentleman' and Smith too is interested in the 'temper and disposition' of his two groups.[2] But Pareto, unlike Smith, does not come out in favour of one group, the entrepreneur. He notes that periods of economic growth favour the entrepreneur, while periods of stagnation or contraction favour the rentier. But he argues that these two élites each have a social function; one to advance change, and the other to resist it. Both functions are necessary. A society ruled by rentiers would stagnate; a society ruled by entrepreneurs would dissolve into chaos. What is needed is a judicious balance between the two. The élites follow their own interests; they do not aim at social equilibrium, but social equilibrium results from their interaction. Each group has conscious aims which affect society, but the two groups are not conscious of their social functions — the unintended consequences of their deliberate actions.[3]

Pareto is brilliant and stimulating but operates at such a general level that the historian may feel he has lost his footing. As a corrective to such 'grand theory', C. Wright Mills wrote *The Power Élite* (1956) and so revived the study of the subject. In this book, written with passion and imagination, Mills studied the political, business and military hierarchies in the USA at the time of the Korean war and emphasised that they 'interlocked', that a 'compact and powerful' élite had come to dominate America, that businessmen and generals influenced key political decisions, and that this was a bad thing. Mills had a good deal to say about the style of life and the attitudes of the élite, and I have tried to emulate him in this respect. However, the controversy which his book raised showed the difficulty of testing the élite theory empirically, for example, of showing that a given élite forms a cohesive group. The fundamental problems of method have been raised lucidly and elegantly by Robert A. Dahl. He defines a 'ruling élite' as a minority whose preferences regularly prevail in cases of conflict over key political issues, which means that one needs (i) a well-defined minority, (ii) conflict situations, and (iii) evidence that the minority regularly prevails, before one can use the term 'ruling élite' at all.[4] This is perhaps to minimize the power of an élite to smother potential conflict—for example, by withholding crucial information—but it is a valuable reminder of the need for methodological rigour.[5] Dahl's solution of the problems of method he raised was to focus on the process of decision-making in a single city, New Haven. From 1784 to 1842, he argued, 'social status, education, wealth and political influence were united in the same hands', in a group he called 'the patricians', men of established New Haven families who were lawyers by profession. In the mid nineteenth century the industrialization of America promoted social change and the patricians were replaced by 'the entrepreneurs', industrialists who had wealth and gained power but lacked high status. As for the twentieth century, Dahl concluded that 'oligarchy' had been replaced by 'pluralism', that 'economic notables' and 'social notables' in New Haven may influence specific decisions, but that there is not very much overlap between wealth, status and power.[6]

The historian of seventeenth-century Europe can learn something from each of these writers, and indeed from other recent work on élites. Mills and Dahl both suggest that one does well to study the overlap between men of wealth, men of status and men of power. From Pareto one can borrow the concepts of 'rentier', 'entrepreneur', 'social system' and 'social function'. Dahl's example also suggested that research on élites might be more manageable if a city rather than a nation was made the focus of attention. In seventeenth-century Europe there were not many cities independent enough politically for this approach to be useful, but two which were independent are Venice and Amsterdam. There were certain obvious similarities between them of which contemporaries were well aware. Thus, in 1600 the Duc de Rohan commented that for wealth Venice was the only rival of Amsterdam, and in 1618 the Venetian A. Donà called Amsterdam 'the image of Venice in the days when it was rising' (*l' immagine della già nascente Venezia*). In 1650, an Amsterdam pamphleteer accused the powerful Bicker family of wanting to take over the Republic and create another Venice.[7] In a Europe mainly composed of monarchies, each was the greatest city of a Republic. In a Europe where the ruling class still tended to identify with fighters, the patricians of Venice and Amsterdam were predominantly civilian. In Pareto's terms, they were foxes in a world of lions. In a Europe whose governing élites usually despised trade, Amsterdam and Venice stood out as places where, at least in the early seventeenth century, trade and politics could be combined with success. The values of the two groups included a stress on tolerance and thrift, two qualities not usually prized by seventeenth-century leaders. In a Europe whose ruling classes tended to spend most of their time on their country estates, the patricians of Venice and Amsterdam lived mainly in town. The economic basis, the ethos and the style of life of the two groups changed in a similar way in the course of the century; the reverse of nineteenth-century New Haven, they began as entrepreneurs and ended as rentiers.

But there were striking differences too. The Venetian élite was one of noblemen, the Amsterdam élite one of commoners. The Venetians were Catholic, the Amsterdammers mainly Protestant. In Amsterdam the nuclear family was the focus of loyalty, but in Venice it was the extended family. But both similarities and differences suggested that systematic comparison might be worthwhile. The comparative approach to history has several advantages. It draws the attention of the historian to what contemporaries usually do not see, for example, the fact that their society is a system of interdependent parts. In this book I shall argue that the Venetian élite, as a nobility, were more oriented toward the family and less towards individual achievement than the bourgeois Amsterdammers; more concerned with display, especially family display, while Amsterdammers set a higher value on frugality, a bourgeois virtue reinforced by their Calvinism. Children brought up in a nuclear family, as in Amsterdam, were more likely to develop a need to achieve than were Venetian noble children, reared in an extended family. Venetians, trained in an old University, Padua, and living in a city which had a glorious past but had ceased to grow, were more likely to prize the old than were Amsterdammers, trained in new institutions like the Athenaeum and Leyden University, and living in a fairly new and rapidly expanding city. Again, the fact that in Venice it was common for only one brother per generation to marry cannot be understood without reference to the system of which this social convention formed a part; the need for birth control not to impoverish the family, the fact that brothers tended to live together in the family palace so that a bachelor was not isolated, the importance of career opportunities for the celibate in the Church and in the navy (for many naval officers married late or not at all).

Comparative history also helps one to see what isn't there. The fact that Venice did not grow in the period and the fact that Venetians did not form joint-stock companies both look more significant when one thinks of the rapid growth of Amsterdam and the importance of the Dutch East India Company. Conversely, the Venetian example makes one ask why the Amsterdammers did not invest more heavily in land and suggests that one might look at Amsterdam's relation to the province of Holland in terms of a city-state dominating the territory round about it.

The comparative approach comes naturally to an outsider, whereas the history of Amsterdam and Venice has been written for the most part by their citizens (often by descendants of the patricians, such as Cicogna, Nani Mocenigo, da Mosto, Elias). Two outstanding examples are Pompeo Molmenti's *History of Venice in Private Life* (1879) and J. E. Elias's *The Vroedschap of Amsterdam* (1903-5). Each was the life-work of its author and a fine example of its kind. Molmenti was concerned with social history, paying particular attention to the patricians, and if he did not altogether escape the defects of the 'old curiosity shop' approach to social history, he was a pioneer in his field. Elias was a political historian who collected information about the genealogy, offices and wealth of every member of the town council; his work is in fact a treasury of under-analysed data. Each wrote with great love of his city and identification with it; it is appropriate that a square in Venice should bear Molmenti's name today. An outsider cannot hope to emulate the virtues of these men. A different approach may at least prevent him from carrying water to the Grand Canal, or, for that matter, to the Amstel.

The remaining chapters will raise and attempt to answer the following questions.

What is the structure of the élite in Amsterdam and Venice? How is it recruited? Is it an 'estate' or a 'class'?

What are its political functions? To what extent does it rule, over whom and by what means?

What is its economic base? Is it rich or poor and where does its wealth come from?

What is its style of life?

What are its most important attitudes and values?

To what extent does it patronize the arts?

How is it trained?

How and why does it change during the period?

The period with which the book is concerned is a long seventeenth century running from about 1580 to about 1720. It is convenient to begin early because the town council of Amsterdam was almost completely replaced in 1578 (the famous *Alteratie*), while in Venice there were important constitutional changes in 1582, a decline in the power of the Council of Ten and its 'junta'. It is convenient to end the seventeenth century rather late because it was in the early eighteenth century that the two groups ceased to be involved in foreign wars, when the Dutch Republic made the Treaty of Utrecht with the French (1713) and the Venetians made the Treaty of Passarowitz with the Turks (1718). There is no other obvious moment to stop till the late eighteenth-century, when the two republics finally came to an end.

The approach adopted in this book is prosopographical. That is, an attempt is made to answer the eight questions listed above by studying collective biography, the biography of 563 men. For Venice the group selected for study was the doges and *procuratori di S. Marco*,† 244 men in all; for Amsterdam it was the 319 burgomasters and members of the town council. In each case the dates chosen were 1578-1719 inclusive. Members of these groups who figure in the text will henceforth be marked by an asterisk. The limitations and dangers of the prosopographical approach have recently been described by one of its leading English practitioners, Professor Lawrence Stone, and his warnings certainly apply to the study of Venice and Amsterdam in the seventeenth century.[8] The most obvious limitation is the one of deficiencies in the data. In the case of the 563 men studied below it has usually been possible to discover something about their families, wealth and political careers, but it is much harder to find out about their taste in painting or their conception of God. A few individuals in each city have left abundant evidence, and studies have been made, for example, of M.A. Barbaro,* Nicolò Contarini,* Lunardo Donà,* Paolo Paruta,* Coenraed van Beuningen,* C. P. Hooft,* Jacob van Neck* and Nicolaes Witsen.*[9] There is a large group for whose attitudes there is some evidence but not so much, and a larger group still for whom there are only a few clues or no clues at all. The obvious danger here is the one about which Stone warns intending prosopographers; of treating the sample about whom there is reliable information as a random sample of the whole population being studied, when it is not. I shall usually start from well-known examples, like the eight men listed above, but try not to assume that they were typical of the rest.

† Discussed on pp. 18-19 below.

In the case of art patronage in Amsterdam, there are good reasons for supposing that the minority about whose patronage we are well informed — Andries de Graeff,* for example, or Joan Huydecoper*— were not typical of the majority of their colleagues in office. In other words, even using the methods of collective biography, it is not possible to generalize on an absolutely firm basis; but to talk about the group without looking at some of its members one by one is to generalize without a basis at all.

Throughout this study I shall refer to the two élites as 'patricians'. The term *patricii* was coined in ancient Rome to refer to the children of the early senators, or *patres*, and so to the members of certain old families. It was revived by humanists in the fifteenth century and applied to urban aristocracies such as those of Nuremberg and Venice, and the term has tended to be used in that sense ever since.[10] In Venice in the seventeenth century the term *patrizii* was used of noblemen in general, while in Amsterdam it was not used at all. However, it will be convenient to use the term 'patrician' in this book to refer to the 563 men who are its subject. How the 563 were chosen will be discussed in the next chapter.

Structure

The greatest problem to be faced in making this study was that of identifying the two élites. However rigorous one might try to be in the analysis of collective biographies, one has to choose the biographies in the first place on the basis of more impressionistic evidence. It is necessary to attempt an answer to the question: what groups had status, power and wealth in Venice and Amsterdam in the seventeenth century? The essential point to make is that Venice was an 'Estate society' in the sense that it was divided into formally defined status groups and that power and wealth tended to follow status. Amsterdam was a 'class society' (much more unusual in seventeenth-century Europe) in that its status groups were defined informally, so that status tended to follow wealth and power.[1]

In Venice the traditional division of society into three estates — the clergy, the nobility, and the rest — was still taken seriously enough to be a social fact. The clergy can be dealt with briefly. As in other parts of Catholic Europe, there was an important distinction between high-status upper clergy — the patriarch, the bishops of the *terraferma* (the north Italian mainland), the *primicerio* or dean of S. Marco — and the low-status lower clergy, such as parish priests and friars. But the upper clergy were usually noblemen, while the lower clergy were usually members of the third estate. The second estate was a legally-defined high-status group. Nobles were those men, women and children whose names were entered in the *libro d'oro*, the golden book. In 1580 this meant, with very few exceptions, that they were descended from people considered noble in 1297 (the famous *Serrata*, or 'closing'). In 1594 there were 1,967 male nobles over the age of twenty-five, omitting honorary nobles like the Este family. In the mid seventeenth century, when the government was in financial difficulties, it became possible for families to buy their way into the nobility for 100,000 ducats a time. In spite of the 'aggregation' of 100 new families by this means, in 1719 there were only 1,703 male nobles over twenty-five, the age at which they entered the Greater Council; a tiny minority of the population of Venice, which in 1720 as in 1580 was about 140,000.[2] Within this estate there were gradations of status. Old families were considered more honourable than new ones, and most honourable were the twenty-four 'old families' (*case vecchie*) who claimed to have been noble and Venetian before 800. However, if processions can be seen in Venice as elsewhere in early modern Europe as materializations of the social structure (which is why struggles over precedence were conducted in such deadly earnest) then it is clear that the fundamental distinction between one nobleman and another from the point of view of status was the offices he held. First came the doge, then the *procuratori di S. Marco*, a kind of life peerage; then the holders of other important political offices. Status and power were closely associated in Venice, and to power we must now turn.

In theory, Venice was governed by a council, the Greater Council (*Maggior Consiglio*), which included all male nobles over twenty-five together with a few under that age. In that sense, status and power coincided exactly. Of course an assembly of some two thousand members was much too big to exercise effective power, and its most important function was to appoint some of its members to office. There was also an upper house, or Senate, which made other important appointments, and could sometimes put pressure on the Greater Council, but even the Senate, with about two hundred members, was too large for effective decision making. To find out who exercised power in Venice it is therefore necessary to look at the holders of key offices. It has been calculated that there were about eight hundred offices in seventeenth-century Venice, and most of them rotated rapidly, changing hands every six months, or eight months, or every year, or every three years. The student of Venetian politics needs to identify the key offices and the men who regularly held them. How does one know a man was powerful? Because he held key offices. How does one know that certain offices were key offices? Because powerful men tended to hold them. The danger of circularity is obvious. It is difficult to do better than contemporaries who thought that important office included ambassadorships, appointments to govern important cities of the *terraferma*, or to be *savio*, or one of the Council of Ten, or to hold a high naval appointment. But concentration on the holders of important offices runs the risk of omitting the latent leaders, the grey eminences who had more power than their offices warranted. Domenico Molin, brother of Doge Francesco Molin,* was said to be such a man.[3]

After status and power the third hierarchy to investigate is that of wealth. A systematic investigation of the wealth of Venetians was

made by the government for tax purposes in 1581, 1661 and 1711.
The historian has reason to be grateful that in Venice, unlike most
parts of Europe, the nobility was subject to taxation. In 1581, according to the tax records, 59 heads of households declared an annual
income from land and houses of more than 2,000 ducats a year.† All
were nobles but three: dal Basso, di Mutti and della Vecchia. In 1711,
70 heads of household declared 6,000 ducats or more annual income;
all were noble but one (Donado Pozzi), though eleven more were
nobles recently aggregated (Bonfadini, Bressa, Carminati, Correggio,
Fini, Labia, Minelli, Papafava, Piovene, Vidman and Zenobio).
Unfortunately for the historian, the tax returns give no information
about wealth which was not invested in land or houses. But virtually
all rich landowners were noble, though many nobles were not rich
men. In Venice as in parts of France, Spain, Poland or Japan, the poor
noble was a well-known phenomenon. Wealth was linked with status
and power because some offices, like ambassadorships, involved their
holders in so much expense that they had to be rich men to accept
them; because rich commoners, from the mid seventeenth century
onwards, were able to buy their way into the nobility; and because
some nobles were able to buy the high-status appointments of
procuratori di S. Marco. In short, there was enough overlap between
status, power and wealth for the historian to talk about a relatively
unified élite.[4]

'Not all the stars of the Milky Way need to be known by the
astrologers, but only the great ones which have influence on this
sublunary world', remarked a contemporary student of Venetian
politics.[5] As a substantial sample of these influential men I have
chosen to concentrate on the twenty-five doges of the period and on
the *procuratori di S. Marco*, henceforth referred to as 'proctors'.
The doge was the official head of state, but unable to take political
initiative: a prince minus the power.[6] Proctors looked after the church
of S. Marco and administered certain charities. They went round
Venice distributing alms, looked after minors and the property of
people who died intestate. They came next to the doge in official
status, and doges were supposed to be chosen from among them (seven

---

† There are enormous problems involved in trying to convert sums like
  these into possible modern equivalents. It is less misleading to compare
  rich and poor within Venice. In 1581 a journeyman builder earned
  about 50 ducats a year.

doges in the period were not). They were exceptions to the rapid turn-over of office in Venice; they were appointed for life and they were senators *ex officio*, though they ceased going to the Greater Council. They were appointed by that council. There were nine 'ordinary' proctors, but 'extraordinary' appointments could be made, and were often made for money, usually from 20,000 to 25,000 ducats. About a third of the appointments in the period were extraordinary ones. In this period there were 237 proctors (and the addition of the seven doges who were not proctors brings the group to be studied to 244). Not all powerful Venetians were proctors, but most proctors were or had been powerful. About three-quarters of them had held high office before appointment, and after appointment their position as permanent senators gave them an opportunity to be influential. Not all rich Venetians were proctors, but the proctors were among the richest men in Venice. In 1581, 9 out of 18 proctors had 2,000 ducats a year or more from houses and land, in other words 50 per cent were from the richest 60 households. In 1711, 20 out of 38 proctors declared 6,000 ducats a year or more, so that over 50 per cent were from the richest 70 households, and about 30 per cent of the richest heads of households were proctors. The increase in their numbers between 1581 and 1711 shows how in Venice, as in England in the seventeenth century, the financial needs of the government led to an 'inflation of honours'. It may be significant that the price of a proctorship was only about a quarter of what it cost a new family to join the Venetian nobility. The great distinction in Venice was between those who were noble and those who were not.

In Amsterdam, the traditional division of society into three estates was ceasing to be useful. Where the Catholic clergy had been seen as a separate estate, the Protestant clergy were regarded as a group of professional men not unlike lawyers and doctors. As for the second estate, Dutch noblemen tended to be found at The Hague (at the court of the Stadholder, when there was one) or in the country on their own lands. The term 'estate' continued to be used by contemporaries, but it changed its meaning as it was applied to different groups within the third estate. Thus C. P. Hooft* in the early seventeenth century referred to people 'of middle or still lower estate' (*van middelbaren ofte noch lageren staet*) as opposed to 'the richest, most honourable and most notable people' (*de rijcksten, eerbaersten ende notabelsten personen*).[7] A pamphlet published at Amsterdam in 1662 expressed shock at merchants and shopkeepers who forget themselves and climb above their estate (*boven sijnen staet treden*), though the writer had to admit that in Amsterdam, merchants included many people of 'power and wealth' (*macht en middelen*).[8] There was clearly a need for a new term to characterize differences in social status in a new way, and the term 'class' was just coming into use in this sense. In the sixteenth century, the Latin word *classis* was used of religious groups in the presbyterian system of church government; in the early seventeenth century it was used of 'classes' of pupils; in the late seventeenth century it was used of tax groups. Spinoza's *Ethics* (1678) contains the statement that men transfer the love or hate they feel towards an individual stranger to 'the whole class or nation whereto he belongs'.[9] An early use of the term 'class' in English also has as its context the social structure of the Dutch Republic.[10] It seems useful to take over this term and to describe the Amsterdam élite as an 'upper class', meaning by this that social status was not defined in legal terms but that in practice men of power and wealth were accorded high status by their fellows.[11] A state of affairs which shocked some foreign observers; in 1586 one of Leicester's circle described the Dutch regent class with contempt as the sovereign lords miller's and cheesemen'.[12]

It remains to see whether power and wealth overlapped in Amsterdam. The men of power are easier to identify than in Venice, because there were fewer offices and they rotated less often. Amsterdam had a Town Council or *vroedschap* with thirty-six councillors (*raadslieden*) appointed for life. There was a sheriff (*schout*), nine magistrates (*schepenen*) and four burgomasters, often but not always members of the Council. The burgomasters were independent of both the stadholder and the Council, which was unusual for Dutch towns and a clue to the political influence of Amsterdam.[13] The burgomasters were appointed by the ex-burgomasters and ex-magistrates for a year, but one of the four served a second term to ensure continuity. Burgomasters and Council together come to 319 men.[14] These men are the 'power élite' of Amsterdam in the period.

The best single source for the wealth of Amsterdammers as of Venetians is the investigation made for tax purposes. There were tax assessments in 1585, 1631 and 1674.[15] The *kohier* or assessment of 1585 shows that the richest and the second richest men in Amsterdam were burgomasters and that about half the Council were among the richest 65 households. According to the *kohier* of 1631,

24 heads of households were worth 200,000 florins†or more (taxation was levied on property, not income). 6 of these 24 were members of the Council (and 7 of the remaining 18 were women or children). According to the *kohier* of 1674, 81 heads of households were worth 200,000 florins or more; 15 were members of the Council, 4 were future members (and 19 of the remainder were women or children). There were rich men in Amsterdam who never entered the Council. Among the richest men in Amsterdam in 1631 were D. Alewijn, G. Bartolotti, and B. Coymans. None of them entered the Council, but their relatives by blood or marriage did. We may conclude that wealth, status and power overlapped to a considerable extent and that we may study the 319 burgomasters and councillors as a unified élite.

An obvious question to ask about elites is how they are recruited. Who chose them? From whom were they chosen? On what criteria?

In Venice proctors were elected by the Greater Council. But how did certain individuals come to be elected? Contarini's famous sixteenth-century description of the Venetian constitution declares that men are elected proctors who have held many offices and are of obvious merit (*una riguardevole bontà*).[16]   Some seventeenth-century writers were more cynical. They suggested that what mattered was money, or family connections (*parentele*) or patronage (*amicitia, adherenze*), in this case presumably the group of clients voting for their patron rather than the patron getting a job for one of his clients. This was the 'tripod' on which political success in Venice was based. This was what mattered in that central informal political institution of Venice, the *broglio*, the meeting of noblemen at St Mark's or the Rialto where the intriguing and bargaining went on before the formal elections in the Greater Council. 'The man with important relatives is honoured and he who is provided with friends is provided with offices'.

It is not easy to say how important these different factors were. Take money, for example. A third of the proctors bought their offices. This does not prove that they would not have been elected anyway; though extraordinary proctors tended to have held fewer important offices than ordinary ones. But to become a proctor it was a great help to have been an ambassador, and only a man of wealth could afford to be an ambassador. To get one's foot on a bottom rung of the ladder

† In nearby Leyden in 1620, a tailor might earn about 80 florins in a year.

of office it was a help to have been to university, and that too cost money. Even 'ordinary' proctors needed wealth.

As for family, a few statistics show its importance clearly. Of the 244, 42 were the sons of doges or proctors; 30 the brothers of doges or proctors; 18, the grandsons; 18, the sons-in-law; 12, the nephews. These figures confirm what contemporaries point out, that there was a small number of wealthy and powerful families within the Venetian nobility, the 'princes of the blood' as they were sometimes called; for example, the Corner family (branch of S. Maurizio), who were known as 'the Medici of Venice'.[18] Members of these families had a better chance of election to office from the time they ran for the junior post of *savio agl'ordini* to the time they tried to become proctors.

As a French observer suggested, the power of these families was exercised through the lesser nobles, 'who are entirely theirs' (*qui sont entièrement à leur dévotion*).[19] Unfortunately very little is known about the links between patrons and clients within the Greater Council and the *broglio*. The voting for and against individual appointments is recorded, but not the names of those who voted. The historian can do little more than collect contemporary gossip; for example, the story that M. Grimani* was elected doge because L. Donà* persuaded his clients among the electors to vote for Grimani; or that Alvise Priuli* was 'a great supporter of his clients' (*assai partigiano dei suoi clienti*).[20]

The factor hardest to measure is, of course, talent. About talent two contrary points need making. The first is that an able nobleman whose family was not wealthy or powerful did have a chance of reaching the top. Perhaps the most spectacular case is that of Nicolò da Ponte,* who began as a poor noble from a minor family, made 150,000 ducats and surprised everyone by his election as doge, aged about eighty-seven. Nicolò Contarini* did not come from a very distinguished branch of his family, and in 1582 he declared an income of only 323 ducats; but he became doge in 1630 none the less. Lunardo Donà was not a member of a powerful family and he declared 326 ducats income in 1582, but he became doge in 1606. On the other hand, seventeenth-century writers sometimes remarked on the number of mediocrities in high office in Venice. One anonymous contemporary (whether a disappointed competitor for office we do not know) said that gifted men sometimes failed to become proctors because they had given offence, while some proctors 'made an impression by their robes and nothing more' (*non fanno altra figura che quella della lor veste*).[21] About 25 per cent of the proctors held no important office before buying their post. Alvise Barbarigo,* for example, described by one contemporary as 'without virtues and without vices, a man who does not speak in the Senate'; by another as 'a good senator and zealous in the public service, but without qualities which really stand out' (*che spicchino di molto*).[22] Of Daniele Bragadin* we learn that he does not hold office and, as far as voting is concerned, 'lets himself be carried along by the current'. But he was a rich man and became a proctor at the early age of thirty-three for 20,500 ducats.[23] Alessandro Contarini* was lieutenant-general to the great Francesco Morosini,* but was described as 'a majestic presence' (*una maestosa presenza*) with nothing inside, like an uninhabited palace.[24]

Not only mediocrity but inefficiency, corruption and even treason were charges made against some of the élite. Zuan Cappello,* at one time *Capitano Generale da Mar*, the supreme naval commander, was imprisoned for a time on a charge of dilatoriness, though he was acquitted. Francesco Morosini,* who had the most glorious naval career of the century, was accused of keeping public money for himself. Zorzi Morosini,* another naval officer, was imprisoned on one occasion for maladministration, but went on to be *Capitano Generale da Mar* all the same, and to be knighted by the Senate for his services. Zuan Pesaro* was tried for his failings as commander against papal forces in 1643, but he ended his life as doge. Zaccaria Sagredo* was deprived of his proctorship in 1630 for abandoning ground to the enemy; five years later he was holding the honourable appointment of *podestà* of Padua. Piero Venier* was imprisoned for challenging a superior officer, and again for leaving the Arsenal when officially on guard, yet he was elected proctor for merit, not money. Jacopo Soranzo* was deprived of his proctorship in 1584 and banished on a charge of revealing state secrets, but he was freed two years later. Which was the miscarriage of justice, the accusation or the pardon? In all these cases the historian may well wonder whether a clique of powerful families could cover up the gravest faults of its members, or whether a powerful man was likely to be framed by his rivals. A contemporary writer suggested that Soranzo, for example, was the victim of envy.[25]

In Amsterdam the formal criteria for appointment to the Council were to be over twenty-five, a citizen, and resident in Amsterdam for the previous seven years. Burgomasters had to be over forty. It was not too difficult to become a citizen in expanding Amsterdam. The population of the city was about 30,000 in 1590; about 90,000 in 1620; about

140,000 in 1640; and stabilized at about 200,000 from 1680 onwards.[26] One could become a *poorter* or citizen of Amsterdam in three ways: by birth, by marriage or by paying a fee—8 florins in 1600, 50 florins in 1650. Over 7,000 new citizens were in fact admitted, at an increasing rate, in the thirty-five years from 1578 onwards.[27] A large number of people were thus eligible for the Amsterdam Council, but vacancies were filled by cooption.

As in Venice, family connections, patronage and wealth all mattered as well as ability. Of the 319 members of the élite, 91 were the sons of other members; 52 were sons-in-law; 44 were grandsons; 10 were brothers; and 9 were nephews. If an individual were councillor, certain close relatives of his (such as brother) were excluded automatically, but there were ways round this rule. The brothers Cornelis and Andries de Graeff* were a powerful force in Amsterdam politics in the early seventeenth century. Cornelis, the elder brother, was a councillor from 1639 to 1664. His brother was therefore excluded; he was in fact elected councillor in 1665, just after the death of Cornelis. But Andries could and did become burgomaster before this. From 1655 to 1662 one of the two was always a burgomaster, and between them they were burgomasters 17 times. The brothers Andries and Cornelis Bicker* were in a similar situation. The elder brother, Andries, was councillor 1622-52 and burgomaster ten times. Cornelis was never a councillor, but he was three times burgomaster. In 1646 seven of the Bicker family held political office at once (minor offices included), possibly a record.[28] The Bicker and de Graeff families were closely allied by marriage. Two daughters of Jacob de Graeff* married two Bicker brothers, and his son Andries de Graeff* married Elisabeth Bicker.[29]

Patronage mattered too. In his autobiography, Nicolaes Witsen,* son of Cornelis Witsen,* tells us that he was appointed to the Council as a result of his friendship with the powerful burgomaster Gillis Valckenier,* and that he was not appointed a magistrate till 1673 because until 1672 the Valckenier faction was weaker than the opposing faction, led by the de Graeffs.[30]

All the same, there were considerable opportunities for new men to enter the council, meaning by 'new men' people whose ancestors had not been burgomasters or councillors of Amsterdam themselves. At least fifteen of the élite were first-generation immigrants to Amsterdam and thirty-three were second-generation immigrants. This group of forty-eight includes eight burgomasters. Adriaen Cromhout* was born in Friesland and Louys Trip* was born in Dordrecht. C. Bambeeck,* A. Pater,* J. Poppen,* J. Munter,* C. van Teylingen* and A. Velters* were all the sons of immigrants to Amsterdam. It is a remarkable fact that of these forty-eight, who came from Calais, from Cologne, from Riga as well as from the Netherlands, only two came from the South. Yet a third of the population of Amsterdam in 1622 were first- or second-generation emigrants from the South. One might regard this as statistical confirmation of the view that Amsterdammers regarded these Southerners with hostility—a hostility expressed in Bredero's famous play, *The Spanish Brabanter.*[31]

Of course, to be new in Amsterdam did not necessarily mean that a man was new to the regent class. There were links between the regents of Amsterdam and those of other cities. Adriaen Pauw* was the son of a burgomaster of Gouda; Claes van Heemskerck* was the son of a burgomaster of Leiden; and Willem Dedel,* the only first-generation immigrant to enter the élite after 1672, was the son of a burgomaster of The Hague. However, it is not difficult to find burgomasters of Amsterdam whose ancestors had not been regents at all. Four famous examples are Jacob Poppen,* Frans Banningh Cocq,* Nicolaes Tulp* and Louys Trip,* and a look at their careers will help to show what opportunities were available at Amsterdam to the politically and socially ambitious.

Jacob Poppen* was the son of an immigrant to Amsterdam who found a job packing herrings. At the age of twenty-seven Jacob married Liefgen Wuytiers, daughter of a former councillor, and the same year he became lieutenant in the civic guard. Three years later he became regent of an almshouse, and in another three he was chosen as a councillor. He ended up a burgomaster.

Frans Banningh Cocq* was the son of an apothecary, an immigrant from Bremen who was said to have been a beggar. But his father married Lijsbeth Banningh, whose family were well represented in the Council in the fifteenth and sixteenth centuries. Frans himself took the name of Banningh, went to university, and when he was twenty-five married Maria Overlander, daughter of Volckert Overlander,* a rich merchant who had been on the Council for the last twenty years. A new man himself, Volckert Overlander* had married a Hooft, one of the most famous families of seventeenth-century Amsterdam. Four years after his marriage Frans Banningh Cocq* entered the Council. He was burgomaster four times, knighted by the King of France, Heer van Purmerland (the estate came through his wife) and he commissioned

Rembrandt's 'Night Watch'. Nicolaes Tulp* was the son of a cloth-merchant, and a doctor of medicine from Leiden. He entered the Council relatively early, at the age of twenty-nine, and was able to celebrate fifty years in it. His second marriage was to a daughter of one of the élite, but he had been a councillor eight years at that point. He was burgomaster four times, though he was sixty-one the first time (in contrast to the new man, Andries Bicker* had become burgomaster when he was forty-one, just over the minimum age). Louys Trip* was much more of an outsider, since he was born in Dordrecht. But he was an extremely rich man, a munitions manufacturer (his mother was a de Geer). He had the favour of the Stadholder (later William III of England) who made him a councillor following his purge of 1672. He became a burgomaster two years later.

The example of Frans Banningh Cocq* illustrates the value to an ambitious family of a systematic marriage policy, while the example of Louys Trip* illustrates the opportunities afforded by political crises. In a similar way to Trip, a group of new men entered the Council in 1578, when supporters of the revolt against Spain took over the government of Amsterdam. Indeed, most of the men in office after the *Alteratie* were new men (the most obvious exceptions are Wilhelm Baerdesen* and Jacob Banningh*) and one of the burgomasters, Adriaen Cromhout,* was, as has been said, an immigrant. His descendants were to be prominent in Amsterdam politics in the next generation.

To sum up. A comparison between the recruitment of the élite in Amsterdam and Venice is complicated by the fact that in Amsterdam one is looking at one process, recruitment to the Council, while in Venice one is looking at two processes — recruitment to the proctor-ship and recruitment to lesser office. All the same some major differences between the two cities stand out. One of them can best be expressed diagramatically.

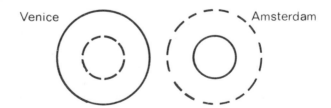

In Venice there was a tightly defined group which was eligible to rule, the nobles, but a more loosely defined inner group who actually ruled. In Amsterdam there was a fairly loosely defined or open group who were eligible to rule, the citizens, but a much more closed inner group who actually ruled. In general, one may say that Venice was a relatively closed society, where for the first half of the period no new families were admitted to the nobility at all. Even after the ennoblements of the mid seventeenth century and after, proctors continued to be recruited from the same old families. The only exceptions are G. B. Albrizzi,* Vincenzo Fini* (the uncle), Vincenzo Fini* (the nephew), Ottavio Manin* and Antonio Ottobon.* Most of the new nobles were immigrants to Venice, usually from the mainland; they were able to buy their way in at the lower level, but not at the higher. Social mobility upwards was difficult in Venice, but so was downward mobility. A poor noble was a noble still. Members of the élite were concerned to help poor nobles. Silvestro Valier* left a fund for thirty noble families in decline, and Ferigo Contarini* was concerned with the foundation of an academy for the sons of poor nobles to receive a fitting education without payment. Amsterdam, on the other hand, was a more open society. Geographical mobility was possible, and an immigrant could become burgomaster. Social mobility upwards was possible. So was downward mobility; five of the élite went bankrupt and had to leave the Council: J. Hooghkamer,* J. Van Neck,* J. Rijn,* and D. Tholincx.* (This point also illustrates the link between wealth and power.) In short, Venice was an estate society, and Amsterdam was a class society.

One might therefore expect the family to be more important in Venice, and the individual in Amsterdam. Statistics seem to bear this out; in Venice 244 élite members came from 66 families, an average of 3.5 each. 13 families had 6 or more members, led by 17 Contarini, 14 Corner, and 13 Mocenigo. In Amsterdam, 319 élite members came from 156 families, just over 2 members each. 6 families had 6 or more members, led by 13 Bickers and 11 Backers. Family seems almost twice as important in Venice. But caution is necessary: 'family' did not mean the same thing in the two cities.

A striking feature of the Venetian nobility as a whole was how few surnames they had between them. In 1594 1,967 male nobles over the age of twenty-five had 139 surnames between them, about 14 individuals to each name. The most common names were Contarini (100 males over twenty-five), Morosini (68), Querini (54), Malipiero and Priuli (52 each).[32] As certain Christian names were extremely popular (there were 7 Alvise Mocenigos in the élite in the period) the possibilities of confusion were great. Even contemporaries made mistakes; in 1607 the Greater Council was unsure which Andrea Vendramin was *podestà* of Chioggia. It is not surprising to find that Venetians tended to use patronymics, but even this did not always prevent confusion. The eighteenth-century antiquarian Cappellari ascribes a diplomatic career to Doge Domenico di Giulio Contarini* which in fact belongs to another man with the same three names.

The crucial question, from the point of view of the study of élites, is what it meant to be a Contarini or a Morosini in seventeenth-century Venice. Historians tend to agree that the unit which mattered was not the group with the same surname (*famiglia*, best translated perhaps as '*clan*') but the branch (*ramo*) or the house (*casa*), the group which lived together in the same place and was usually named after its situation. Thus there were Corner members of the élite from five different branches—S. Cassian, S. Luca, S. Maurizio, S. Polo, S. Samuele—named from the parishes in which they lived. Some branches of a clan might be rich, while others were miserably poor. One must not assume that members of the same clan voted the same way in the Greater Council and elsewhere. In the celebrated conflict between 'old' and 'young' in the later sixteenth century, Alberto Badoer supported the former while Ferigo Badoer supported the latter.[33]

However, I should like to argue that the solidarity of the clan has been somewhat underestimated. It shared a coat of arms, a point which mattered in the seventeenth century. When a certain Girolamo Corner, from a minor branch of the clan, was condemned to death for treason in the early seventeenth century, the major branches offered 100,000 ducats, no small sum, to get him off, presumably to keep the clan name untarnished.[34] Some Correr wills prescribed that any woman in whom a given branch of the clan would become extinct must marry another Correr to keep the wealth within the clan.[35] There is no doubt that some branches of major clans knew that they were related to certain other branches, and this fact is likely to have made for solidarity between them. The crucial question is whether a Venetian nobleman is more likely to have voted for another nobleman of the same surname in elections to office, other things being equal. This question cannot be answered directly, but it is suggestive that there were five Contarini doges during the period, from different branches. That is, they formed less than 5 per cent of the nobility but 25 per cent of the doges. An anonymous writer of the mid seventeenth century discusses the leading figures in Venetian politics and their assets, and emphasises the support that their relatives give to certain members of the Contarini, Zustinian, Mocenigo and Morosini families—among the biggest surname groups of all.[36] He writes of Girolamo Zustinian, for example, that 'as far as public elections are concerned, he depends on the ring-leaders (*caporioni*) of the Zustinian family', a phrase which can hardly refer to one branch alone.

In private life the branch was certainly the unit, and its organization merits further description. It was not a nuclear family. Characteristically it was a group of brothers living in a palace with their wives and children. When a nobleman married he would tend to bring his wife to the palace, the building which symbolized the branch and held it together. Noblemen in their wills exhort their sons not to split up to form more branches; Antonio Grimani* even told his sons to keep a common kitchen and a common table.[37] It is difficult to be precise about the average size of the branch or house. A list of 1714 mentions 216 noble families, 667 houses (*case*) and 2851 males.[38] This would mean an average of just over 4 males to a branch. Presumably there would be as many women: unmarried girls living at home, and wives of the men. And of course the household would include servants too. Some branches were clearly much bigger than this. At least 45 members of the élite had 4 sons or more surviving infancy (girls tend to be under-reported in genealogies) and at least 60 proctors had 4 or more brothers each. But even the average branch was clearly bigger than the average Venetian household, which had 3.7 members in the 1580s, and 4.5 members in 1642.[39]

Wills make many references to the 'honour of the house' (*l'honorevolezza della casa*). These words were not empty ones. The house was able to make considerable demands on the individual. A dramatic example is that of patriarch Zuan Dolfin, who began his career in the church but had to leave it because of the 'interests of his family'; he was needed to look after his younger brothers when his father was employed outside Venice.[40] Girls might be put into nunneries to save on their dowries, and men might not marry because this was the most reliable means of legitimate birth control. 30 per cent of the élite never married, and the figure for the nobility as a whole in the same period is about 60 per cent.[41] Venetian noble families, like noble families elsewhere, faced a dilemma. Too many children living in the style to which the family was accustomed risked the impoverishment of the house. Hence the growing use of *fedecommessi* (entails) which tended to establish primogeniture at one remove; younger sons were provided for but their children were not. The effect was to discourage them from marrying, but this risked the extinction of the house for lack of male heirs. It was difficult to find a strategy which avoided the two dangers of impoverishment and extinction. The Venetian nobility as a whole came nearer to the second danger, and declined from 1,967 males over twenty-five in 1594 to 1703 (in spite of the aggregations) in 1719. The élite, who tended to be richer than the average noble, married more frequently, but a number of the leading figures in this period were bachelors. Nicolò Contarini,* Lunardo Donà,* Francesco Erizzo,* Francesco Molin,* Francesco Morosini,* Nicolò Sagredo* are all examples. The cases of Erizzo,* Molin* and Morosini* are a reminder of the obvious career for a noble bachelor outside the church—the navy.

The Venetian 'house' may be described as a 'collateral' type of family organization. The relationships which tended to be stressed were brother-brother and uncle-nephew. There is plenty of evidence of this within the élite. Pasquale Cicogna* was very close to his brother Antonio. Lunardo Donà* was close to his brother Nicolò, who moved into the doge's palace when Lunardo was elected. Zuan Bembo,* another bachelor doge, was close to his brother Filippo, with whom he was buried and to whose sons he left his property. Nicolò Donà* was close to his brother Francesco and to Francesco's sons. The division of labour between brothers was a way in which the house could further the political career of one of its members (financial assistance was another). Battista Nani* was able to devote his energies to politics because his brother Agostino took over the running of the household, and Nicolò Contarini* was in a similar situation. The Senate recognised this 'special relationship' between brothers when it knighted Girolamo Corner* for the services of his dead brother Cattarino. The traditional form of trade organization in Venice, the *fraterna*, institutionalized the same relationship. No doubt this bond between brothers contributed to the development of huge kin groups or 'clans' like the Contarini.

There is much less to say about the family in Amsterdam, but this is significant in itself.[42] Trading companies were composed of individuals, not of families. Brothers traded for themselves. The four sons of Gerrit Bicker* all went into trade but they divided the world between them and each kept to his area. Grown-up sons often lived in separate homes. The brothers Andries and Cornelis de Graeff* lived in the same street, the Heerengracht, but in different houses, and they had different country houses too. Entails were known to the Amsterdam élite but they seem to have been less important than in Venice—another sign of 'individualism'. A dead man's property would simply be divided among his children. Tax assessments in Amsterdam read very differently from those in Venice. In Venice a nobleman declares that he lives with his brothers in the family palace and then declares the family property, adding his 'speciality' or individual property if there is any. In Amsterdam individual brothers and even sisters would be assessed separately. Thus in the *kohier* of 1674, six members of the de Geer family, a man and five women, are assessed at 217 florins each. They had their financial independence. Property and housing are not everything but at least they are valuable clues to a family structure. The general impression is one of individualism in the sense of sons being independent of their fathers during their lifetime, and of younger sons being undependent of their elder brothers. Even daughters might show an independence unusual elsewhere. To take an example from nearby Delft, where the affair became a *cause célèbre*, burgomaster Geraldo Welhock had to make great efforts to prevent his daughter marrying the man of her choice against his will, and the couple did marry after his death.[43] The tax records suggest that the rich widow who was head of a household was an important Amsterdam phenomenon.

In short, one may say that in Amsterdam the nuclear family was dominant—man, wife and unmarried children. In Venice, the dominant form of social organization was the extended family, covering several generations and including the married male children. In Venice, the 'joint family' was dominant: residence was joint, so was consumption, and so was ownership. There was much more stress on the family in Venice than in Amsterdam. Families went back much further, whereas in Amsterdam it was difficult to take genealogies back earlier than the fifteenth century. Amsterdam was, after all, a fairly new city, its élite were not noble and were only just taking to the use of surnames in the sixteenth century.

The Venetian social system seems to have been oriented more towards the family, the Amsterdam system towards achievement. In Venice it was possible for men from certain families to become doge without really trying. Alvise Contarini,* Carlo Contarini,* and

Domenico Contarini* are all examples. No one at Amsterdam, not even the Bickers, had greatness thrust upon them in quite this way. In short, the distribution of wealth, status and power was made on different criteria in Venice and Amsterdam. The Venetian élite was part of a legally-privileged estate of noblemen with considerable loyalty to their extended families. The Amsterdam élite was an informally defined governing group, part of a class rather than part of an estate, more individualistic and more achievement-oriented, attaching less importance to family loyalties (particularly in the first half of the period) and defining 'family' in a much narrower way.

Political Functions

In Venice the élite ruled not just a city but an empire by sea and land. Crete and the Morea were the remains of the maritime empire (Cyprus had been lost just before the period began). The empire on the mainland or *terraferma* included between 1,500,000 and 2,000,000 people, some living in sizable towns. Brescia had about 40,000 inhabitants in the mid-seventeenth century, Padua about 30,000, Vicenza about 25,000.[1] Venice, in other words, was not so much a city as a territorial state, and the running of this state involved the élite in a variety of functions. It may be useful to distinguish four main functions, central government, local government, war and diplomacy, and to look at the offices held by members of the élite, at least the more important offices.[2]

A hundred and fifty-one of the élite held important office in the central government as members of the College, the Senate, or the Council of Ten. The College was a group of 26 men; the doge, his 6 councillors, the 16 *savi*, and the three heads of the *quarantia*. Five of the *savi* were particularly concerned with the mainland, and 5 were young men learning the art of government. The heads of the *quarantia* were judges. The senate was concerned in particular with decisions about war and foreign policy, and the Council of Ten was concerned with crime.

A hundred and eleven of the élite held important office in local government, the government of the empire. Subject cities were left their own laws and even their own town councils, but nobles from Venice were sent to govern them. Important cities had two *rettori* ('rulers'); a *podestà*, concerned with civil matters, and a *capitano*, concerned with military ones. The most honourable of these posts was *podestà* of Padua. One might compare the Venetian *rettori* with the French *intendants*, especially since their reports on the state of the region they governed were not the least important part of their jobs. The *provveditori generali* of Palma and Candia were more or less viceroys, governing Friuli and Crete respectively, and so they are included here rather than with the military appointments.

Seventy-five of the élite held important military or naval office. The Venetian élite was not composed entirely of 'foxes'. Famous examples of 'lions' are Zuan Bembo,* Francesco Erizzo,* Francesco Molin* and, most celebrated of all Francesco Morosini.* They were elected doge after distinguished military careers, holding such offices as *capitano in golfo*, looking after the Adriatic; *generale contra Uscocchi*, appointed to root out the Uskoks, Christian refugees from the Ottoman Empire turned pirates, operating from Senj and elsewhere on the coast of Dalmatia; *provveditore d'armata*, in command of a fleet, and *capitano generale da mar*, the naval commander-in-chief, appointed only in time of war (*provveditore generale da mar* was the highest peacetime appointment). The navy was a normal career for a Venetian nobleman and two posts on each galley were reserved for adolescent nobles. But they did not monopolize officer posts; for example the Dane Curt Siversen was *tenente generale* in 1660. The land forces were not officered by Venetians. At the top one would usually find great nobles from other parts of Italy, such as Luigi d'Este, an infantry commander in 1614, or Alessandro Farnese, prince of Parma, who commanded the Venetian cavalry in the mid seventeenth century. One might find a foreign nobleman, like John Ernest of Nassau, commander of Dutch mercenaries in 1617. Below them, the officers were mainly nobles from the mainland.[3]   But Venetian nobles were attached to the army to supervise the professional commanders, as 'field commissioner' (*commissario in campo*) without whose consent the commander could not act, or, at the highest level, through the office which Francesco Erizzo held four times, that of *provveditore generale dell'esercito in terraferma*.

Seventy-four of the élite were ambassadors at one time or another. Of the four fields, this is the one which seems most obviously dominated by the elite. Diplomats had a good chance of becoming proctors, and proctors had a good chance of being appointed diplomats. This is what one might have expected; diplomats in seventeenth-century Europe had to be men of high status and considerable wealth. About 25 per cent of the élite held no important office at all. The wealthy music-loving Marco Contarini* is an example. It is unlikely that he wanted to hold office.

A point which needs emphasis but does not receive it from the figures quoted so far is the number of times members of the élite held important office. Girolamo Zustinian* was *savio del consiglio* thirteen times. If a man was appointed an ambassador once, he was likely to be appointed several times. Anzolo Contarini,* for example, was twice ambassador to Rome, twice to England, once to France, and once to the Emperor Ferdinand III. Members of the élite might hold two or three offices at once. Agostino Nani,* for example, was appointed proctor in 1612. In the five years 1612-16 he held office fifteen times. Thus in 1612 he was a *savio*, an ambassador extraordinary, and 'reformer of studies' of the University of Padua.[4] This spread of offices in a single year is a reminder that in Venice, the four main political sectors—central government, local government, war and diplomacy —were not exclusive of one another. Like the traditional Chinese mandarin or English civil servant, the Venetian patrician was an all-rounder rather than a specialist, an amateur rather than a professional. Nine of the élite held important office in all four sectors and 47 held office in three of them. There was a place in the political system for the specialist in naval affairs, like Francesco Morosini,* and a place for the financial expert, like Zuanfrancesco Priuli,* governor of the mint, who was elected proctor because he discovered how to redeem the public debt. But distinctively Venetian is the minority of all-rounders, including doges Lunardo Donà,* Francesco Erizzo,* Antonio Priuli* and Bertucci Valier.* Donà was ambassador to Spain, *capitano* of Brescia, *savio*, and *provveditore generale di terraferma*. Antonio Priuli* commanded a galley, joined the Council of Ten, was sent as ambassador to France, and was appointed *capitano* of Padua. Two distinguished diplomats, Battista Nani* and Simone Contarini,* were asked to be *capitano generale da mar*, the supreme naval appointment, without having had naval experience. Both refused, but what is significant is that they should have been asked at all. Nicolò Contarini* held his first military appointment at the age of sixty-four, in the war against the Habsburgs in 1617.[5]

There were offices which involved the administration of the city, and members of the élite held them, but they were relatively unimportant. For example there were the *provveditori di notte*, who dealt with security in Venice. The proctors themselves had civic functions, such as almsgiving, but this was no longer an important part of their job. The city had been transformed by becoming the centre of a territorial state.

To use the language of 'political functions' risks giving a false impression. The élite were not completely disinterested servants of the public. Many of them wanted power and as a group they exercised power at the expense of other people. A zero-sum conception of power is as necessary to the historian or political scientist as a functional conception. Excluded from power were three groups; the lower nobility, the commoners of Venice, and the subject population, noble and commoner, of the Venetian empire.

The lesser nobility were not, in theory, excluded from power at all.[6] The traditional view of the Venetian constitution (of which the most famous expression is the sixteenth-century treatise by Gasparo Contarini) was that it was a mixed constitution, in which the doge represented the monarchical element, the Senate the aristocratic element, and the Greater Council the democratic element. In the early seventeenth century, Traiano Boccalini also emphasised that Venice was a meritocracy in the sense that any noble could aspire to high office.[7] Not everyone accepted this view, though it may have functioned as an ideology helping to maintain the élite in power. Jean Bodin, with his gift for penetrating below the surface of political reality, argued in the later sixteenth century that Venice had been in turn monarchy and democracy but that it had 'changed into an aristocracy, and that in such quiet sort, that it was not well by any man perceived that the estate was at all changed'. Similarly, an anonymous treatise on the government of Venice, written about 1660, declares that Venice is an oligarchy which conceals the fact (*oligarchia . . . in modo . . . segreto e latente*).[8]

To decide this question in a satisfactory manner it would be necessary to make a statistical study of elections to a wide range of offices over a long period, a study better undertaken by a group than by an individual historian. The more provisional conclusions of the last chapter were that it was not impossible for an able nobleman who was not from a rich or powerful branch of his family to enter the élite, but that it was much easier for the wealthy and the well-connected, that the contemporary distinction between an upper nobility (the *grandi*) and the rest had substance. The lesser nobles resented their exclusion from power and on occasion worked together against the *grandi*. The constitutional conflict of 1582, when the Council of Ten and its 'junta' lost power over foreign policy and finance to the Senate, was to some degree a conflict between greater and lesser nobility; the continuance of the junta was supported by 'the greater senators with their clients and relations'. In the late sixteenth century the Venetian nobility came near to splitting into two groups. Several different conflicts came near to fusion; an older generation, the *vecchi*, versus a younger, the *giovani*; the greater nobles versus the lesser; supporters of Spain versus supporters of France; the devout versus the anti-clerical.[9] Another example of 'the lack of harmony that is seen nowadays between the

greater and the lesser nobles' (*i grandi e la nobiltà minore*) was the conflict between the Senate and the Greater Council in 1656. The Senate
appointed Antonio Bernardo* to be *capitan generale da mar*, but the
Greater Council chose Lazzaro Mocenigo instead.[10] But the most
famous example of the lesser nobles as a force in politics in the period
is to be found in the early seventeenth century, in the movement
associated with Renier Zen.* [11]

In 1625 the wealthy and pious Zuan Corner* was elected doge. He
favoured his relations more than was customary for doges to do, and
he was attacked by Zen,* who went on to describe the enormous gulf
between the greater and lesser nobles. Zen* had the ear of the Greater
Council; on one occasion he rose, spoke for four hours and was heard
with 'marvellous attention'; a contemporary estimated that nearly two-
thirds of the Greater Council belonged to his 'faction'.[12] It was said that
he wanted to depose the doge, and the danger was taken seriously
enough for one of the doge's sons to try to assassinate him in 1627. The
faction of the poor nobles declared that they were unable to enter the
Council of Ten, and demanded entry. In fact all that happened was a
minor change to the position of the Council of Ten; Zen's* election
as proctor (1628); and, when Zuan Corner* died in 1629, his succession by Nicolò Contarini,* who was not one of the *grandi* and who was
elected with the help of the votes of the supporters of Zen,* another
candidate in this election.

The Zen* movement is extremely revealing of the structure of
Venetian politics, as open conflicts often are. In the first place, it is in-
teresting to find that the leader of the poor nobles was not one of them.
Renier Zen* was not elected a proctor till his movement was well under
way, but he was well connected, allied to important branches of the
Barbarigo and Contarini clans, and he had already served as an
ambassador in Savoy and Rome before 1625. In the second place, we
here see how the lesser nobles were able to put pressure on the greater.
In the third place, it can be seen how limited this pressure was.
One naturally wonders why the movement of the lesser nobles fizzled
out so easily. One possible explanation is in the strength of cross-
cutting social ties. The 'horizontal solidarity' of poor nobles and rich
nobles was balanced by the 'vertical solidarity' of patrons and clients.
Zen* had his clients, but Corner* had his. A lesser noble would be torn
between allegiance to his social group and allegiance to his patron. As
modern social anthropologists like to point out, conflicting allegiances
are often a force making for social cohesion, because a man caught

in such a conflict has a strong interest in seeing that any given dispute is settled by a compromise.[13]   Cross-linking of this kind may well be the fundamental reason for the relative absence of political conflict in Venice. It is also a reminder not to exaggerate the cohesiveness of the élite.

There is less to say about the ways in which the élite was able to exclude from power the commoners of Venice and the subject population of the mainland. 'Divide and rule' seems to have been their fundamental maxim. The commoners of Venice can be divided into the citizens and the rest. The citizens were some 5 per cent of the population of Venice, in other words, they were not very much more numerous than the nobles. They were excluded from the Greater Council, but their ambitions were satisfied in a number of ways. Certain offices were reserved for them; the Grand Chancellor, the secretaries to the Council of Ten, to the Senate, and to ambassadors. If an ambassador died *en poste*, his secretary might take over. These posts (apart from secretaries to ambassadors) were for life. Given the rapid rotation of office among the nobles, the secretaries were in a position rather like senior civil servants as compared with ministers in Britain today. Some of them appear to have enjoyed considerable power. It was said that the secretaries of the Council of Ten supported the continuance of the junta in 1582; their power was threatened by the reform movement. Renier Zen* denounced the rule of the secretaries, perhaps thinking in particular of Zuanbattista Padavino, secretary to the Council of Ten from 1584 on, whom he thought responsible for a sentence of banishment passed on him.[14]   One of the few new families to enter not only the nobility but also the élite in this period, the Ottobon, were a family of citizens who had served as chancellors or secretaries. One late-sixteenth-century writer, Botero, also suggested that the guilds or *scuole* helped satisfy the citizens by drawing them and the nobles together.[15]

Robbed of their natural leaders, the citizens, the 'many-headed monster, the plebs' was less dangerous. Gasparo Contarini explained the absence of conflict between nobles and common people in Venice by impartial justice and a regular corn supply. Doges and proctors threw money to the people when they were elected. The old custom of the election of a fishermen's doge, who was solemnly received and kissed by the real doge, might be seen as a device for persuading the people they participated in a system from which they were in reality excluded. One seventeenth-century writer was cynical enough to suggest that the government encouraged the two factions of the common people, the *Castellani* (from Castello, the sailors' quarter) and the *Nicolotti* (from S. Nicolò, the fishermen's parish) with their annual fist-fights, in order to keep the people divided.[16]

Similar devices were used to control the nobles and the common people of the mainland, with varying degrees of success. As Botero pointed out, the privileges of the cities of the mainland were not abolished under Venetian rule.[17] Local noblemen could still become town councillors. The Venetian *rettori* deliberately fraternized with the local nobles. Some of them became Venetian nobles too. The Savorgnan, a powerful family from Friuli, had done so before the period began, and the 'aggregations' of the later seventeenth century included the Angarani, nobles from Vicenza; the Bressa, nobles from Treviso; the Ghirardini, nobles from Verona; and many others. Nobles from the mainland could and often did make a career in the armed forces of the Republic.[18]

These concessions apart, local nobles often continued to exercise considerable power in practice. The *rettori* held office for too short a time to get to know, let alone control, their areas. To take just one example. Count Francesco Martinengo Colleoni was a power to be reckoned with near his castle of Cavernago, in the Bergamo area, early in the seventeenth century. He had men killed with impunity. The Council of Ten issued instructions for his arrest in 1619, but the *rettori* did not carry out this order, writing to excuse themselves that 'Cavernago is a strong place with moat and drawbridge so that hundreds of men would be needed to surround it . . . there is armour for a hundred and a number of arquebuses.'[19]

In the mainland too, the Venetian government seems to have adopted a policy of 'divide and rule'. When Francesco Erizzo* was administering Friuli, he is said to have advised the government to make some nobles counts but not others in order to prevent them presenting a united front. The seventeenth-century *Opinion*, once attributed to Fra Paolo Sarpi, warns the Venetian government against Padua, Verona and Treviso and suggests that 'it is convenient to make show of administering justice impartially to them, but never to let slip any occasion of humbling them', and that, if the leaders of the discontented can be identified, 'let all occasions be laid hold on for exterminating them . . . it will be more prudent to employ poison instead of a hangman, because the advantage will be the same and the hatred the less.' Discontented nobles there certainly were, for example, a certain Paulo Zagallo at Campolongo in 1646, who declared that the Venetians were 'long-nosed busybodies' (*becconazzi fatudi*) and that he would prefer to live under Spanish rule. One wonders how many people thought like him but were too cautious to say so; he was banished for his outburst. But another possible alliance, to the advantage of the Venetians, was between *rettori* and common people of the mainland against the local nobles, as at Brescia in 1644.[20] Once more we see that cross-cutting conflicts led to relative stability.

In Amsterdam, by contrast, the political functions of the élite, especially their official functions, were narrower in range. They were city-oriented. A list of the main offices makes this clear. Besides the burgomasters and councillors, there was one *schout* (or sheriff), nine *schepenen* (or magistrates); there were treasurers, ordinary and extraordinary (the number varied within the period); masters of the orphans (*weesmeesteren*); masters of insurance (*assurantiemeesteren*); commissioners for marital affairs (*huwelijksche zaken*), maritime affairs (*zeezaken*), the exchange bank (*wisselbank*); the lending bank (*bank van leening*), the excise (*accijns*), and bankruptcy (*desolate boedels*). At the end of the period, the office of postmaster became a desirable one. To be a commissioner was for many a step on the ladder leading to the Council and even the burgomastership. Nearly 20 per cent of the élite administered almshouses at some point in their career, before or after becoming councillors: the *Leprozenhuis*, for example, the house for lepers; or the Sint Joris Hof; or the houses of punishment for men and women, the *Rasphuis* and the *Spinhuis* respectively.

At first sight the military functions of the Amsterdam élite appear much more important than in Venice. Nearly two-thirds of the group were officers in the civic guard (the *burgerij* or *schutterij*), usually ensigns or lieutenants before becoming councillors, and reaching higher ranks after they had joined the élite. It is important not to take membership of the civic guard (perhaps 'trained bands' would be a better translation) too seriously. Indeed, thanks to painters like Rembrandt and van de Helst one cannot forget that the civic guard, at Amsterdam and elsewhere, was more of a club than an effective military institution; that its officers were more able to brandish a fork or a wineglass than a sword or a halberd. On one of the rare occasion that they were really needed, the French invasion of 1672, the Dutch *schutterij* were not particularly effective.[21] The institution looks like a good example of the play element in culture, so well

analysed by Huizinga.[22] The impression is confirmed when we find
Dirk Munter* (the son of a burgomaster, and a burgomaster himself
later on) as an ensign in the civic guard at two years old. Similarly,
in the early eighteenth century, two sons of burgomasters were
appointed captains of infantry in the Amsterdam garrison at the ages
of five and nine respectively.[23] Such offices were a way of rewarding
clients as well as relatives. A contemporary attack on the Bickers
accuses them of inserting their men as officers of the civic guard.[24]

One must not take the military activities of the élite too seriously,
but one must take them seriously enough. It is easy to scoff at
merchants dressed up as soldiers, and at a civic guard which did not
defend anything. One needs to remember the importance of the
schutterij in the coup of 1578, when the new men and the religious
exiles took over the government of Amsterdam, and one must not
forget that some members of the élite knew about fighting. Before
they entered city politics, J. E. Huydecoper* was an ensign of foot and
Ferdinand van Collen* a cornet of dragoons. After his bankruptcy
Diederick Tholincx left Amsterdam and joined the army. Dirck Bas,*
Ferdinand van Collen* and Nicolaes Witsen* were 'field deputies'
(civilian supervisors of military operations not unlike the Venetian
commissario in campo). The sons of Pieter Hasselaer,* Dirck de
Vlaming,* and Cornelis van Vlooswijck* all took up military careers.
There were also naval officers in the élite, such as Jacob van Neck,*
Laurens Resel,* and Wijbrand Warwijck.*

The political functions of the Amsterdam élite do not look very
grand compared to the Venetian. However, the contrast was not as
great in practice as it was formally. Indeed, it may be argued that the
Italian model of a city dominating the *contado*, the country round
about it, is a useful one for understanding the position of Amsterdam
in the seventeenth century.

At the most precise and least important level, it is worth drawing
attention to the fact that the Amsterdam élite exercised certain rights
over pieces of nearby countryside. The burgomasters were permanent
feoffees (*erfleenheeren*) of certain manors (*ambachtsheerlijkheden*).
Amstelveen is a well-known example, and Gerard Schaep* certainly
thought that Amsterdam's rights over Amstelveen were not to be
despised.[25] In a similar way, the office of bailiff (*drost*) of the nearby
castle of Muiden was in the gift of the burgomasters, and C.P. Hooft*
obtained it for his son, the poet and historian who made the
'Muiden circle' (*Muiderkring*) of such importance in Dutch cultural

history. F. H. Oetgens* had his son made *poldermeester* or official in
charge of the polders near Amsterdam.

However, to call Amsterdam a 'city-state' is to say something more
important and more vague. The resolutions of the council show that
the councillors did not spend all their time talking about almshouses.
At the beginning of the eighteenth century, they spend a good deal of
time talking about the Spanish Succession and the value of a defensive alliance between the Dutch Republic, Britain, and Sweden.[26]
Why? Because, to over-simplify, the councillors ruled Amsterdam,
Amsterdam ruled Holland, and Holland ruled the United Provinces.
In theory the Dutch Republic was a federation in which the seven
provinces were equal, and in theory Amsterdam was only one of
eighteen towns in the province of Holland, but in practice the
Amsterdam élite had ways of getting what they wanted. After all,
Amsterdam paid about 44 per cent of the taxes of the province
of Holland, and the province of Holland (from 1612, when the quota
was fixed) paid 57 per cent of the taxes of the whole Dutch Republic.
In other words, one city paid 25 per cent of the taxes of the whole
nation. This point about the predominance of Amsterdam is often
made, but it may be useful to approach the problem through the
collective biography of the élite.[27]

Amsterdam sent representatives to certain institutions of the province of Holland. In the first place, to the States of Holland. There were
19 deputations to the States, one from the nobility of the province (the
Ridderschap) and one each from eighteen towns. A town deputation
usually consisted of a burgomaster or ex-burgomaster, the town
pensionary (or legal adviser) and some other members of the Town
Council. However many people made up the deputation, the town had
one vote. First the nobility voted, then Amsterdam, which gave the
Amsterdammers a chance to make their views prevail among the
waverers. Four towns were usually independent of Amsterdam in their
policies—Dordrecht, Haarlem, Delft and Leyden. But the lead of
Amsterdam was usually followed by the thirteen smaller towns, such
as Alkmaar, Hoorn, Gouda or Schiedam, and thus the policy of
Amsterdam became the policy of the States of Holland. Then there was
the Council in Committee (*Gecommiteerde Raaden*) of the province
of Holland, which dealt with taxation and defence. It was divided into
two colleges, for the North and South of the province. Of the ten
members of the college of the Southern Region (*Zuider-Kwartier*),
one was always from Amsterdam. Fifty members of the élite held
office in the Council in Committee in the period. Other important

offices in the province were filled by members of the élite. Thus Gerrit
Delft* was Treasurer-General of Holland in 1580. Fifty-one members
of the élite held office in a local admiralty, usually Amsterdam or
Zeeland.

The province of Holland in turn sent representatives to certain
federal institutions, of which the most important were the States-
General (in which the seven provinces had equal representation) and
the Council of State (*Raad van State*), which had twelve members, of
whom three were from Holland. To the States-General went fifteen
burgomasters and councillors such as Wilhelm Baerdesen,* Reynier
Cant,* Andries Bicker,* Nicolaes Witsen* and Jacob Valckenier.* To
the Council of State went fourteen of the élite — Reynier Cant,*
Vincent van Bronckhorst, Hendrick Hudde, Jacob Hinlopen,* for
example. This last duly was a particularly demanding one, and Bronckhorst* and Hudde* both resigned from the Town Council when they
were appointed; they had to spend too much time in The Hague.
Similarly, Coenraed Burgh* resigned to take up the important federal
appointment of Treasurer-General of the Union.

It has more than once been suggested that appointment to these
posts outside the city was a kind of banishment for leaders of a losing
faction in the Town Council. As C. P. Hooft* put it, 'To the college of
the Council in Committee in The Hague ... were sent ex-burgomasters
that people seemed to want to do without here' (*dye men schijnt hyer
liefst te willen missen*). The argument from chronology supports this
suggestion. Gerrit Witsen* was sent off in 1617, after criticising the
policies of the powerful F. H. Oetgens.* Cornelis Bicker* was sent in
1651, just after the Prince of Orange had had him removed from the
Town Council. Henrick Hooft* was sent when the opposing
Valckenier faction were in power, and when Hooft* came to the top
again in 1672, it was the turn of Gillis Valckenier* to be sent to
the Council in Committee.[28]

However, it may still be argued that membership of these provincial
and federal bodies helped the élite to influence, if not to dominate, the
rest of the Republic, in matters of foreign policy in particular. Members
of the élite sometimes played a crucial political role in Dutch affairs;
indeed, the Union of Utrecht, from which the United Provinces
derived, was negotiated in part by one of them, Reynier Cant, *
councillor first to William the Silent and then to Maurice of Nassau.
It was in the important years from 1646 onwards, when peace negotia-
tions were in progress, that the powerful Andries Bicker* headed the
Holland deputation to the States-General. Their role as diplomats was

another means by which members of the élite were able to influence the affairs of the whole United Provinces, so that the trading interests of the Amsterdammers were reflected in the foreign policy of the Republic. 24 of the élite served as diplomats in the period.[29] At the time of the war between Denmark and Sweden in 1644, for example, the ambassadors to these two powers were Andries Bicker* and Gerard Schaep.* Albert Burgh* was ambassador to Russia and to Denmark. Joan Huydecoper,* hampered by his ignorance of German, was ambassador to Brandenburg, and so on.

Another means whereby Amsterdam and its élite were able to influence the rest of the Republic was via the East and West India Companies and the Society of Surinam. Like the Republic, these companies had a federal structure. There were regional 'chambers', each with their directors, from whom were chosen the directors of the company as a whole, the XVII of the East India Company (Vereenigde Oost-Indische Compagnie or VOC) and the XIX of the West India Company. Eight of the XVII always come from Amsterdam. However, Amsterdam never had an absolute majority of the XVII, and the meetings of the VOC were held at Middelburg as well as at Amsterdam. In practice, once again, the power of Amsterdam was greater than it was on paper. The Amsterdam chambers of the VOC and the West India Company were by far the most important. Amsterdam put up 57 per cent of the capital of the VOC at its foundation. Amsterdammers infiltrated into the other chambers, whether as an insurance policy to protect their investments or to gain control. In the late seventeenth century, Amsterdammers owned about 38 per cent of the capital of the Zeeland chamber of the VOC, for example.[30]   In 1719, A. Velters* had 74,000 florins invested in the Delft chamber of the VOC. At any rate, 103 of the élite, about 30 per cent, were directors of the VOC or the West India Company or the Society of Surinam. This meant Amsterdam influence on the government of an empire much more far-flung than that of Venice. Of 18 Governors-General of the Netherlands Indies, 1609-1718, 3 came from Amsterdam regent families. Laurens Reael,* son of a councillor, ruled the East Indies from 1616 on and later entered the Town Council himself. Coenraed Burgh* left it to become Governor of Curaçao.[31]

In 1650, a pamphlet expressed the fear that 'the great fish Amsterdam might eat up the smaller ones', and that the rulers of Amsterdam (the

Bickers in particular) had designs to make themselves the rulers of the state, and create another Venice. Hysterical in tone, exaggerated in its claims, this pamphlet expressed a fear of the élite which had some basis in reality.[32] But how much basis? To answer this question we need to follow Robert Dahl's advice and to identify situations where there is a conflict between Amsterdam and the rest of the Republic. For example, in the 1590s, leading Amsterdammers were engaged in the trade with Spain, although the Republic was at war with Spain at the time. The ships taking corn to Spain sailed under false flags. In 1596 there was a conflict between the States-General, which forebade the export of corn to Spain and Italy, and the rulers of Amsterdam, who objected; it was Amsterdam which won.[33] Although the town council of Amsterdam had declared on 22 March 1607 that peace meant 'the irreparable damage and decline of these lands', they could not prevent the Twelve Years' Truce, which lasted from 1609 to 1621. However, the Amsterdam élite were able to involve the Dutch Republic in the war between Sweden and Denmark in 1644, when the Dutch ambassadors to the two belligerents were burgomasters of Amsterdam. Their aim was to force the king of Denmark to lower the tolls he levied on Dutch ships passing through the Sound.[34]

In other cases, as so often in politics, conflict situations were complicated by the fact that more than two groups were involved, as will be seen by taking some famous examples of conflicts in chronological order. In 1618, Jan van Oldenbarnevelt, Grand Pensionary of Holland, was tried and executed for treason. This was the climax of the conflict between Oldenbarnevelt and the Stadholder,† Maurice of Nassau, a clash of a peace policy with a war policy, and of a relatively tolerant form of Calvinism with an intolerant form. Some of the Amsterdam élite had come into conflict with Oldenbarnevelt, who supported Le Maire's Australian Company, a competitor with the VOC, and opposed the foundation of a West India Company when the question was discussed about 1607. One of Oldenbarnevelt's judges was Reynier Pauw,* a burgomaster of Amsterdam, a fiery Calvinist, a founder-member of the VOC and interested in the West Indies trade as well.

†The Stadholder was a kind of Dutch doge, a nobleman (from the house of Orange) who was head of state in most of the United Provinces, a survival into republican times of the nobles who governed provinces on behalf of a prince.

But not all the Amsterdam Town Council supported Maurice of Nassau; indeed he purged the council in 1618, removing eight men and replacing them with his own appointments.[35]

Maurice's successor as Stadholder, Prince Frederick Henry, once declared, 'I have no greater enemies than the town of Amsterdam.' He clashed in particular with burgomaster Andries Bicker.* The Prince wanted centralized control over the local admiralties, Bicker* opposed him. The Prince wanted to forbid the sale of ships to Spain, Bicker* and his colleagues Abraham Boom* and Jan Geelvinck* engaged in this trade. The Prince wanted to continue the war with Spain, Bicker* wanted to make peace, as was finally done in 1648. Following the peace, there was a clash between the rulers of Amsterdam and the new stadholder William II, because Amsterdam wanted to reduce the army, and the stadholder did not. It was this conflict which led to the most spectacular confrontation in 1650, when William II sent an army against Amsterdam to depose the 'Bicker league'.[36]

In the period without a stadholder that followed William's death, the most powerful man in the Republic, the Grand Pensionary, Jan de Witt, was allied to the Amsterdam élite through his marriage to Wendela Bicker. When William III became Stadholder, in 1672, clashes with Amsterdam began again. In that year he removed ten men from the Town Council, including the Bicker ally Andries de Graeff*, replacing them with his nominees. In spite of this purge, clashes between Amsterdam and William continued to happen in the 1680s, when Amsterdam supported a peace policy and opposed the levy of troops.[37]

These conflicts would be an excellent means of testing the power of the élite if only it had been cohesive. In fact it was split into parties, or (to use a term with fewer misleading modern overtones) into factions.[38] The Prince of Orange was able to purge the council in 1618 because he had the support of the faction led by Reynier Pauw, * and his successor was able to carry out a similar coup in 1672 because he had the support of the faction led by Gillis Valckenier.* Unfortunately we do not know very much about these factions, and it is particularly hard to answer the important question; was the conflict between factions a conflict over policies, or just a struggle for office? Differences of opinion between burgomasters or councillors were not recorded in the minutes of meetings.[39] In one case we do have good evidence of a conflict over policy, in the key area of urban redevelopment.[40] C.P. Hooft* attacked F.H. Oetgens* and his friends for the 'private profit' they made in real estate thanks to their inside knowledge due to their political position. In a few other cases we know about religious conflicts.[41]

However divided in other respects, the élite were united in their fear of 'the mob' (*het grauw*). An undated late seventeenth-century report by the colonels of the civic guard deals with the measures to be taken in the event of rioting or plundering. In 1617 the houses of some leading Amsterdammers, Arminian in religion, had been attacked and plundered, possibly with the encouragement of their religious opponents. Amsterdam was a port, and so liable to be the scene of sailors' riots, as it was, for example, in 1624, 1628, 1652 and 1696. After the de Witt brothers had been done to death by a crowd in The Hague in 1672, the Amsterdam élite must have slept less soundly at night. But it was not part of their style to distract the many-headed monster with carnivals or by scattering money when burgomasters were elected, as Venetians did. For the preservation of public order, they simply relied on the civic guard.[42]

In both Amsterdam and Venice there were clashes between centre and circumference, metropolis and empire. But the comparison is complicated by the fact that one cannot refer to Amsterdam as the 'centre' without qualification. It may have been what the Habsburg pamphleteer Lisola called it, the *primum mobile* of Holland, but The Hague was its rival as the centre of government of both the province and the federation. It was in The Hague that the States of Holland, the Council in Committee, the States-General and the Council of State all met. The Hague was also the seat of the stadholder's court. The doge was part of the Venetian élite, but his Dutch equivalent, the stadholder, was quite outside the Amsterdam élite and sometimes clashed violently with it. The same must be said of the Grand pensionary.

It is clear that the governing élites of Venice and Amsterdam were not just town councillors. They dominated empires. The Venetians ruled the 1½ to 2 million people living on the mainland. The Amsterdammers dominated the 700,000 inhabitants of the province of Holland, if not the 2 million inhabitants of the whole United Provinces. This dominance was institutionalized in Venice through the *rettori* of the subject cities. It was a less formal kind of influence in the case of Amsterdam. Burgomasters might go on embassy and naval officers enter the council, but the city did not control either diplomacy or the navy, as was the case in Venice. In its political as in its social structure, Venice was a more formal society, Amsterdam a more informal one.

Economic Base

In his famous study of the circulation of élites, Vilfredo Pareto distinguished 'rentiers' from 'speculators' (or entrepreneurs). This distinction was partly made on the basis of attitude—rentiers were defined as unimaginative conservatives, entrepreneurs as imaginative innovators. It was also made in terms of two contrasted economic bases. Rentiers are men on fixed incomes; entrepreneurs are men whose incomes vary with the efforts they make to pursue profit. This may be a case of economic determinism, but it need not be. A variable income is likely to stimulate the imagination, but then a man who enjoys innovating is likely to prefer opportunities for profit to an income which is fixed. In this comparative case-study of élites, it is obviously important to find out whether Venetians and Amsterdammers were predominantly rentiers or predominantly entrepreneurs. It would also be useful to know how wealthy the two groups were relative to one another and relative to other groups in the two communities.

To discover the wealth of the Venetian élite and the sources from which it was derived, there is no better evidence than their tax-returns.[1] Venetians paid the *decima*, a tenth of their annual income from 'movable goods', essentially houses and land. The *decima* was assessed in 1581, 1661 and 1711 (in fact it should have been assessed much more often) and the returns made by each head of household still survive. Although the inhabitants of the mainland paid a different tax, Venetians paid the *decima* on their property in the mainland too, so (cheating apart) a fairly complete picture of their land and houses should be given by this source. Even the head of state had to declare his income, a procedure surely unique in Europe. In 1581, the doge and 17 proctors returned their income; in 1711 the doge and 37 proctors did so. They represent virtually the whole élite at the beginning and at the end of the period, hence I shall assume that they represent a fair sample of the whole. They were not an economic group in themselves, but most of them belonged to the group of large property owners.[2]

The land, to take this first, tended to come in scattered pieces.

This may have been deliberate policy, to insure against local disasters to crops. Venetians owned land most of all in the Padua and Treviso areas, near at hand, but they also owned substantial amounts near Vicenza and Verona; in the Polesine (towards Ferrara); and as far away as Friuli (towards Trieste). Estates tended to be broken into tiny fragments. Marco Contarini's* estate at Piazzola, for example, was divided into a hundred and eleven parts. The estates were cultivated by the local peasants, usually for a fixed rent in kind but sometimes for a money rent or on a share-cropping basis, which made difficulties for the landowners compiling their tax-returns; they had to calculate their average income over five years. Leases tended to be short, for five years or less.[3] The crops grown included wheat, rye, sorgum, millet, oil, wine and, towards the end of the period, maize, or *sorgo turco* as it was usually called. There are many references in the documents to chickens and pigs, often as *regalia*, or customary presents from tenant to landlord; but there are a few references to other livestock.

Urban property consisted of houses and shops in Venice, or more rarely in other towns, such as Padua. It ranged from palaces let to fellow-nobles to tiny shops, like the hat-shop on the bridge at the Rialto owned by Lunardo Donà.* On the whole it seems to have been less important than land.

As for the amount of income derived from these sources, the 18 members of the élite who declared their income in 1581 averaged about 1,300 ducats a year each, from Marco Grimani* at 330 ducats to Gerolamo da Mula* at 3,300. The 38 élite members of 1711 averaged 7,500 ducats a year each, from Piero Zen* at 1,257 ducats to Alvise Pisani* at 35,000; inflation had considerably decreased the value of the ducat by this time.[4] One might contrast these sums with the 70 ducats a year probably earned by a journeyman mason in Venice in the early seventeenth century.[5] In fact the contrast was still greater, because the tax-returns are not concerned with 'movable goods' (*beni mobili*). Movables included silver, jewels and money deposited in the Mint for safe-keeping (and 5 per cent interest) or invested in business, or lent to private individuals, and declared as 'leases' (*livelli*).[6]

A certain amount of information about movable goods can be gleaned from wills. A few examples will suggest the importance of the money deposited at the Mint. It is referred to in the wills of Zuan da Lezze* (died 1625), Antonio Grimani,* who made his will in 1624 and told his heirs to leave the money there; Alvise Barbarigo* (died 1678), Gerolamo Basadonna* (died 1697), whose wife's dowry,

12,000 ducats, was deposited there; Alvise da Mosto,* (died 1701)
who had deposited the vast sum of 39,000 ducats; and Ferigo Corner*
(died 1708). Unfortunately, wills rarely refer to the total wealth of
the testator, so that there is no way of calculating the relative
importance of movable and immovable goods in the wealth of the
élite.[7]

It is mainly from wills that the historian can glean a little information about the trading activities of patricians.† A few were involved
in trade with the East of the traditional Venetian kind. At the beginning
of the period, Antonio Bragadin* had agents at Aleppo and Tripoli
and Zuan Francesco Priuli* had one at Istanbul; at the end of it,
Alvise Mocenigo* had agents at Istanbul. Two proctors from the
Foscarini family (*ai Carmini* branch) were definitely engaged in trade,
Giacomo Foscarini* and his son Zuanbattista Foscarini.* Paolo
Paruta* was involved in the trade with Alexandria. Agostino Nani*
and Zuanne Dolfin* were both involved in the Syria trade.

It is interesting to find Antonio Bragadin* and Giacomo Foscarini*
arguing in their official capacities for Venetian involvement in the
spice trade in 1584. Zuanbattista Foscarini* was involved in the
trade in woollen cloth, which was of increasing importance in seventeenth-century Venice. He carried the business on through a factor.
In 1624 Antonio Grimani* had 12,000 ducats invested in a soap-
works, and he exhorted his heirs to remain in the business. In
1660 Almoro Tiepolo* set up a company to trade in silk in partnership
with Salamon Annobuono, a Jewish merchant. In the later seventeenth
century Domenico Contarini* had 2,000 ducats invested in a business
with the Foscoli brothers, who were not nobles. What the Venetians
did not do was invest in joint-stock companies. The dominant form
of business organization was still the family, even if investments
were accepted from outside, as in the example just quoted.[8]

The élite can also be found trading in the produce of their estates,
an activity practised by nobles in many parts of seventeenth-century
Europe, from England to Russia. Nicolò Donà* was engaged in the
grain trade; Zorzi Corner, the son of Zuan I Corner,* sold cattle
and grain, Antonio Priuli* was in the timber business. Indeed, given
the amount of land which was leased out by them for rents in kind,

† It should be noted that all but three of the examples quoted come from
the period before 1624. For changes in the economic activities of
patricians, see chapter 9 below.

the majority of the élite must have engaged in this sort of trade, if only at second hand through a steward or manager.

Members of the élite acquired their wealth by inheritance; by trade, in a few cases at least; by marriage; and through the profits of office. In Venice, as elsewhere in early modern Europe, a wife came with a dowry. In the social group which we are discussing, a dowry in this period might be anything from 5,000 to 200,000 ducats. The last figure is that of the dowry of Franceschina Dolfin, who married Girolamo, son of Antonio Priuli,* in 1618. To marry into the family of a reigning doge (as Priuli* was at the time) was an expensive business.[9] One way of increasing the dowry was to marry below one's status, outside the Venetian nobility. Ten members of the élite did this during the period. For example, Zuanbattista Corner* married Zanetta Noris, whose family came from Brescia; and Benetto Soranzo* married a doctor's daughter, Maria Flangini.[10]

The profits of office might be ecclesiastical or secular. The ecclesiastical are better known. Campanella went so far as to say that 'the greater part of the nobility of Venice live from canonries and bishoprics'. He was making anti-Venetian propaganda and he was exaggerating, but he did have a point to exaggerate.[11] Some members of the élite retired from political life to enter the Church, like Pietro Basadonna,* who became a cardinal, and Zuanne Dolfin,* who became cardinal and bishop of Vicenza. But since in Venice a branch of a noble clan tended to pool its resources, one needs to look also at the benefices landed by the brothers, uncles and nephews of the élite. Particularly successful in this respect were certain branches of the Grimani, Corner and Dolfin clans. It was said that the brothers Francesco Grimani,* Zuanbattista Grimani* and Zuan Grimani* were all supported by their relative the bishop of Bergamo. Another bishop of Bergamo was Ferigo Corner, son of doge Zuan I Corner,* and between 1577 and 1722 seven out of ten bishops of Padua came from the Corner clan. From 1657 till well after the end of the period, the archbishop of Udine was always a Dolfin.[12]

Historians have tended to place less emphasis on the possible profits of political office, but they were important too, and not just the judicial offices of the *quarantia*, whose salaries were a well-known form of poor relief for impoverished noblemen. The offices held by members of the élite included some with high salaries. In the early seventeenth century, five senior naval officers received over 10,000 ducats each a year.[13] Ambassadors received from 5,000 to 7,000 ducats a year. It is true that these posts involved their holders in expenses, but also true that over and above the salaries there were considerable perquisites and opportunities for profit. The difficult thing is to estimate this unofficial income. Official sources are naturally silent, while contemporary comment may well be ex-aggerated. It seems worth recording all the same that in the seventeenth century observers remarked on the 'modern alchemy' which was converting offices from a source of loss into a source of profit; that it was said that in the war with the Habsburgs in 1617, some leading nobles enriched themselves with public money; that the great Francesco Morosini* was twice accused, in 1663 and 1670, of keeping public money for himself.[14] One mid-seventeenth-century writer even drew up a list of the profits, as distinct from the income, of offices, and mentioned among the most profitable the *governatori delle entrate*, supervising direct taxation; the *provveditori al sale*, administering the government's salt monopoly, an important form of indirect taxation; the *provveditore* of Corfu (worth about 12,000 ducats a year); the *provveditore* of Zante, worth 20,000 ducats a year; and, most important of all, the *bailo* or ambassador to Istanbul. He did not have to present accounts, but he was given money to bribe the Grand Vizier. One writer thought he might make 100,000 ducats in three years, or even more if he was greedy; another, that he was the only official 'who can rob without scruple'.[15]

After this general survey of the resources of the Venetian élite, it is time to raise the general question: were they entrepreneurs or were they rentiers? Of a small number, one can say with some con-fidence that they were entrepreneurs in the sense of being involved in trade and interested in profit; Antonio Bragadin,* Giacomo Foscarini,* Antonio Priuli* are examples who have already been quoted. Others, like Alvise da Mosto* and Ferigo Corner,* with considerable sums deposited in the Mint, can reasonably be classified as rentiers.[16] But all we know of the majority of the élite is that they owned considerable amounts of land.

Owning land does not necessarily make a man a rentier (in the sense that the term is used throughout this book); what matters is a man's attitude to the land, whether active or passive, whether he is interested in 'projects of improvement' (as Adam Smith put it) or is content to sit back and wait for his steward to collect the rent. Some of the élite certainly had an active attitude to their land: Marcantonio Barbaro,* for example, owner of the famous villa Maser, designed by Palladio and decorated by Veronese. Barbaro's* was a slightly unusual case in that he had virtually no property in Venice and virtually no other land. Of the 1,000 ducats a year which this estate brought him, 60 per cent came from leasing it out and the high proportion of 40 per cent from the direct administration of the demesne.[17] Ferigo Contarini* was interested in agriculture. A certain Africo Clemente, notary of Padua dedicated a treatise on the subject to him in 1572, and Ferigo Contarini* also headed a consortium of nobles for the development of the area round Treviso. In the early seventeenth century, Girolamo Corner* was involved in land reclamation.[18] In 1550 a third of the mainland was uncultivated, and much was marshy, but around 1600 noble syndicates for draining the marshes were extremely active. Canals were dug and bridges were built. Much improvement was done by means of forced labour imposed on the local peasants by their Venetian rulers, the beneficiaries being the Venetian noble landowners.[19] In some cases one can watch individual members of the élite laying acre to acre. Luca Michiel* bought 69 *campi* of land at Meolo in 1607, and 11 more *campi* in 1610.[20] One unfriendly observer gave what one might call an 'imperialist' explanation of acquisitions like these, suggesting that the Venetian *rettori* 'skinned' the subject population of the mainland, and that Venetian nobles usurped the common lands and defrauded widows and orphans.[21] It is certainly the case that between 1646 and 1727, about 90,000 hectares of common land in the mainland was sold off, and that nearly 40% of this amount was bought by Venetian nobles.[22] It is obviously difficult to be sure of the rights of the matter in any individual case. For example, Antonio Barbarigo* had an estate at Casale, near Montagnana, in the Padua area. The commune complained that he had taken some of the common land 'on which we poor peasants are able to pasture our swine'. The case was heard by noble judges in Venice, and judgement given in Barbarigo's* favour in 1690, a year in which he held the office of *provveditore delli beni inculti*, concerned with uncultivated land in the *terraferma*.[23]

It is also possible to find members of the élite with a relatively passive or rentier attitude to their lands. Throughout the period, members of the élite employed managers or stewards to look after their estates, as one might have expected, given the size of some estates and the need for their owners to live in town most of the year for political and other reasons. Africo Clemente, in his treatise on agriculture (which went through eight Italian editions between 1572 and 1714) recommended Venetians to provide themselves with 'skilled and experienced managers' (*fattori pratici et esperti*), and to pay them well, insisting that they be professionals and not servants used to other work such as looking after the horses. It is likely that this advice was taken and that the seventeenth century saw the increasing importance and professionalisation of the estate manager. Evidence of professionalisation is the fact that a certain Giacomo Agostinetti published a book of instructions for such estate managers in 1679. The author boasts that he is a 'thoroughbred steward' (*fattore di razza*), having served for forty-five years in the Veneto, and his father having been a steward before him. He is concerned with estates large enough to need a head steward with subordinate bailiffs (*castaldi*) under him. He gives the impression of highly rationalised estate management, singing the praises of double-entry book-keeping and recommending landowners to keep coloured drawings of their estates with each piece numbered so that they can visit their land without leaving Venice. On the question of the control exercised by the owner, Agostinetti is, as one might have expected, somewhat ambivalent. He suggests that the living quarters in the villa should not be too near the peasants, which means noise, nor too far, or the owner will not be able to keep his eye on things. He goes on to praise the Venetian senator who did not care whether he bought land near Padua or near Treviso: 'It doesn't matter to me whether my income comes to me along the Brenta or along the Sile'—a rentier attitude if ever there was one.[24]

It is clear from the wills of some members of the élite that they employed stewards to manage their estates. Francesco Corner* (died 1584) had had his Cyprus estates administered by *fattori,* not altogether honestly. He recommended his heirs to look after the estates in person. On the other hand, Alvise Barbarigo* made a special bequest to the *fattore* of his villa at Merlana for good and faithful service. It must not be assumed that absentee landlords meant estates without improvements. The stewards of the Tron property at Anguillara near Padua in the mid eighteenth century reclaimed land and improved ploughing techniques. But comparing the Venetians with other noble landowners in Europe, the absence of treatises on agriculture written by noblemen and of noble agricultural societies is remarkable.[25]

If it is not clear exactly how much interest members of the élite took in the details of estate management, it is still less clear how they treated their peasants, who slept in the stables or lived in straw huts while their masters lived in palaces. The peasant question is discussed in two treatises on agriculture written in the seventeenth century for noble landowners in the Veneto. G.B. Barpo, a voluble clergyman from Belluno, suggested that an estate would be a delight if it were not for the peasants, who are vicious, envious, proud and obstinate. Agostinetti, who has already been cited, took a more moderate line. He knew that some peasants water the wine or cheat in other ways, but recognised that there are good peasants too. Generosity on the landlord's part is a good investment: 'good landlords have good workers'. His attitude to the peasants is essentially manipulative. In one place in his book he discusses the choice of ploughs and the choice of tenants together; the peasant too was a tool. One commentary on the Venetian noble landlord may be read by anyone who cares to browse through *il Barbaro*, the famous Venetian collection of family trees with notes on the lives of individuals. Not infrequently he will come across the laconic entry: 'murdered by the peasants' (*ammazzato da' contadini*). [26]

In the case of Amsterdam, tax-returns (*Kohieren*) are again the best single source for examining the wealth of the élite. [27] There were assessments in 1585, 1631, 1674 and 1742. The tax was the 'two hundredth penny', 5 per cent of property. In 1585, 65 individuals or households were assessed at 50 florins or more. 18 élite members, about half, belong to this group, and the men with the highest assessments in Amsterdam were burgomaster Dirck Graeff,* who paid 210 florins, and burgomaster Wilhelm Baerdesen,* who paid 200 florins. In 1631, 100 individuals or households were assessed at 500 florins or more, meaning that they were supposed to be worth 100,000 florins or more. 16 of these were members of the élite, and the largest fortune, 500,000 florins, was declared by the heirs of the late burgomaster Jacob Poppen.* In 1674, 259 individuals or households were assessed at 500 florins or more; they included 35 members of the élite, of whom the richest was Joan Corver,* worth 419,000 florins. Seven years later he became burgomaster. There was no reassessment after this till 1742, when an income tax replaced the previous property tax. 103 people declared an income of 16,000 florins or more, and 27 members of the élite belonged to this category. Burgomasters D. Trip,* J. Six* and L. Geelvinck* were the second richest, third richest and fifth richest individuals respectively.

Of course the historian cannot accept these tax-returns at their face value any more than tax-returns in Venice or anywhere else. In a few cases the returns can be checked against other sources—and found wanting. Jacob Poppen* left 920,000 florins when he died in 1624, but his heirs were assessed at only 500,000 florins in 1631. Dirck Bas* was assessed at 100,000 florins in 1631, but left 500,000 florins in 1637. The 240,000 florins declared by E. Trip in 1674 were only 20-25 per cent of his real wealth, according to a recent study. On the other hand, some of the amounts which appear in the returns may have been exaggerated. Andries de Graeff* was assessed at 292,000 florins in 1674. But the assessment was the work of his political enemies G. Valckenier* and Nicolaes Witsen.* De Graeff* knew they were out to get him, and changed his residence, moving to Utrecht to escape Amsterdam taxes, but this device failed. Presumably it was a supporter of his faction who stuck a paper on the Town Hall, inscribed 'Matthew 17.24-27'. St Matthew says that 'Jesus asked Peter, of whom do the kings of the earth take custom or tribute? Of their own children, or of strangers? Peter saith unto him, Of strangers. Jesus saith unto him, Then are the children free.'[28] The gaps between assessments allow some extremely rich men to slip through the net, like the two millionnaire burgomasters Alexander Velters,* who left over a million florins when he died in 1719, and Jeronimus de Haze,* who left over three million when he died in 1725.

Amsterdam tax records, unlike Venetian ones, do not say how a man's wealth was made up. For this it is necessary to have recourse to other kinds of source.[29] From these it appears that the Amsterdam élite invested in houses, land, ships, stock and bonds. One result of the great expansion of Amsterdam in the seventeenth century was the inflation of the price of houses, which were often divided among several owners. Thus Josias van de Blocquery* owned 5/32 of a house in Amsterdam. Houses were a safe but not enormously profitable investment. One estimate, in 1622, was that they brought in 3 per cent per annum.[30]

Land, like houses, brought in the safe but slender profit of 3 per cent per annum.[31] About 30 per cent of the élite appear to have owned some land, but it is not altogether clear what the land was used for. The pattern seems to differ in each of the few cases where some of the details are known. Joannes Hudde* was described as a 'cattle breeder' (*ossenweider*). All the same he did not own very much land, just over 4,000 florins' worth. The biggest piece was about 15 *morgen* of land near Sloterdijk, just outside Amsterdam, which had peasant houses on it. Did the peasants look after his cattle?[32] Fredrik Willem van Loon* had a farm, 'Treslong,' but also small pieces of land which seem to have been rented out as 'residences,'[33] Marten van Loon's* land, unlike the others, carried manorial rights. Jacob de Graeff* had his manor of Zuidpolsbroek administered by a steward (*drossard, rentemeester*); I do not know if this practice was a general one.[34]

A third possible investment was in ships, popular in the late sixteenth and early seventeenth century. When Cornelisz Joriszoon* married Grietge Backer in 1588, he was worth 24,000 florins, of which 2,000 was invested in ships, that is, in trading ventures.[35] In the early seventeenth century, with the rise of the VOC (the United East India Company), this form of investment was replaced by stock (*actien*). Stock was not a safe investment in a period and a city when speculation on the Stock Exchange was already a fine art, but there was the possibility of enormous profits. When Admiral Piet Hein captured the Spanish silver fleet in 1628, the West India Company paid a dividend of 50 per cent. As for the VOC, its success may be measured from the fact that Nicolaas van Bambeeck* at his death in 1722 held 'old stock' of the VOC of which the face value was 21,000 florins; their true value was assessed at 146,000 florins.[36] To decrease the risk, owners of stock distributed their holdings between different companies and different chambers of the same company. Alexander Velters* held stock in the VOC (Amsterdam chamber) and the West India Company (Amsterdam chamber) but also in the Delft and Enkhuizen chambers of the VOC. Jeronimus de Haze* invested in the English South Sea Company as well as in Dutch companies.[37]

A fourth form of investment was in bonds, (*obligatiën*) that is in loans, usually to the city of Amsterdam or the province of Holland. This was said in 1622 to bring in 5 per cent or 6 per cent a year, nearly twice as much as houses or land; but in 1679 Amsterdam was paying only 4 per cent interest.[38] The VOC also borrowed money in this way. One method of investment in the public debt was the purchase of *rentebrieven*, or annuities, which could be bought and sold like stock. One kind of annuity—the *losrente brief*—was specifically redeemable. Another kind was the life annuity, which expired on the death of the holder.

It is obviously important to know in what proportions the wealth of the Amsterdam élite was distributed between these four forms of investment. Unfortunately, it is possible to give a precise answer to this question only in a small number of cases, and most of them (15, to be exact) are from the early eighteenth century. From these cases it appears that a typical investment pattern for a member of the élite about the year 1700 would have been to invest about half his wealth in bonds; about 32 per cent in stock; 12 per cent in houses; and 6 per cent in land. More scattered pieces of evidence from the early seventeenth century suggest that about the year 1600, land was a much more important form of investment, accounting for about 30 per cent of wealth. Bonds were much less important. Shares were held in specific voyages of specific ships. (For the evidence on which this paragraph is based, see the Appendix.)

Since they were not noblemen, members of the Amsterdam élite were often described by occupation, so that it is possible to say something about how they made their money as well as how they invested it.[39]   Nearly half were described as merchants of some kind: herring-merchants, like Cornelisz Joriszoon,* Gerrit Delft* or C.P. Hooft;* Hooft* was also a grain-merchant, like Jacob Coppit* or Claes van Vlooswijck.* These were the traditional Amsterdam occupations and so was timber-merchant (Harmen van de Poll* and his son Jan van de Poll*) and rope-merchant (Pieter Boom,* Jan Verburch); or soap-boiler, like various members of the Spiegel family; or brewer, the occupation in which the Bickers made their money. About 1600 these occupations were the dominant ones, but then the pattern began to change.[40]   Some members of the élite were quick to move into the new, dangerous and profitable trade with the Indies. Gerrit Bicker* was moving from brewing into the East Indies trade before his death in 1604, and Hendrick Hudde* was already involved in this trade as early as 1594. A third of the élite were directors of the VOC, or the West India Company, or the Society of Surinam. Towards the end of the period banking became an important occupation, at least part-time banking combined with trade, as in the case of Balthasar Scott* or his father Everard Scott,* or Daniel Hochepied,* or Jean Deutz.* Printing and bookselling became important in Amsterdam in the course of the seventeenth century, and the king of Amsterdam printers was surely Dr Joan Blaeu,* whose press on the Bloemgracht was the largest and most up to date in Europe. He was map-maker to the VOC, and also involved in the shipping of slaves to the plantations of Virginia.[41]

Fourteen members of the élite are described either as 'seller of diary produce' *(zuivelkooper)* or 'stockbreeder' *(ossenweider)*. One might call them entrepreneur landowners. Stock-raising meant importing lean cattle from the Holstein area, fattening them and selling them to feed the growing population of Amsterdam—an occupation which was increasing in importance, if we can argue from the fact that in 1660 the market for Danish cattle was moved from Enkhuizen to Amsterdam.[42] This group includes Balthasar Appelman* and Joannes Hudde.* If it is added to the merchants, then the two together would include over half of the elite. Another form of entrepreneur land-drainage schemes, notably the draining of the Purmer and the Beemster. Of the 16 original head-landholders *(hoofd-ingelanden)* of the Beemster in 1608, four were members of the élite: Pieter Boom, * Barthold Cromhout, * Jan ten Grootenhuis* and Jacob Poppen. * This spectacular and profitable undertaking (most remarkable for the use of windmills in a land-drainage scheme) may help explain how Jacob Poppen* and others (p. 56 above) had as much land as they did.[43]

Thirty, or just under 10 per cent, of the Amsterdam élite were professional men: lawyers in the main, like three advocates from a single family, Cornelis Cloeck,* Nanning Cloeck* and Pieter Cloeck,* but there were also a few doctors, Martin Coster* and Nicolaes Tulp* being the most famous examples. So was Jan van Hartoghvelt,* for whom his political opponents once arranged a sick-call so that he would miss a crucial meeting of the council. There were also some naval officers, of whom the best known is Jacob van Neck.* Thirty-nine of the élite were directors of companies but not described as merchants or lawyers; it is difficult to know whether to see them as businessmen or bureaucrats. 77, or just under 25 per cent, of the élite had no occupational description at all. There is danger in arguing from this negative evidence, but in a number of cases we also have positive evidence that these men were what their contemporaries called *renteniers*, men who lived from the interest on their bonds. These 'renteeners' (as Sir William Temple translated the Dutch term) are classic cases of what we call 'rentiers'. They included F.W. van Loon,* Jacob Bicker* and Nicolaas van Bambeeck.*

The most striking feature of this brief survey is surely that, although the Amsterdam élite were defined in the first instance by political criteria, more than half of them have turned out to have been concerned with trade, and a third to have been connected with the East and West India Companies. There is no doubt of the connection between the economic basis of the élite and some of their political attitudes. There are powerful individuals of whom one might say, not unfairly, that they behaved as if the business of the United Provinces was business and as if what was good for the VOC was good for the Dutch Republic. The ties between business, politics and war were even closer than the ties C. Wright Mills found in the 'power élite' of the USA in the time of the Korean war. The munitions manufacturers on the Amsterdam town council included Reynier Cant,* Louys Trip* and Gillis Sautijn* (the last two inserted by Stadholder William III and favouring his war policy when the majority of the town council favoured peace). Abraham Boom* and Jan Geelvinck sold ships to Spain in the early seventeenth century, and Andries Bicker* supplied silver to Spain which was used to pay Spanish troops in the Netherlands. No wonder the town council commented in 1607 that peace would be the ruin of 'these lands'.[44]

The last question to ask about the economic basis of the Amsterdam élite is whether they were rentiers or entrepreneurs. The question is a difficult one because it involves not only a pattern of investment but (as remarked in the case of the Venetian élite) a set of attitudes. Burgomaster F.H. Oetgens* owned a good deal of urban property. A man who lives on the rent of houses looks like a rentier, but in fact Oetgens* was an expert and unscrupulous speculator in real estate. He was *Stadsfabriekmeester* of Amsterdam, planning urban development. He bought land outside the city walls near the Haarlem Gate, and then planned the expansion of the city in just that direction, so that his property increased greatly in value. C.P. Hooft* protested against what Oetgens* was doing, and wanted the city to take over the land, but Oetgens* kept it.[45]   No wonder an Amsterdam wit called part of the city 'Jordaan', 'the promised land', and the name stuck. Again, Jacob Poppen* with his investments in land looks like a rentier, but he was very much involved in 'projects of improvement', draining the Beemster. Oddly enough, it looks as though the Amsterdam élite were most entrepreneurial in attitude when they were most involved with land, in the early seventeenth century, and that the retreat from land into bonds and the rise of 'rentier' attitudes occurred together.

To sum up: the one thing which it ought to be possible to compare precisely in the two cities is wealth, but it is in fact difficult to say which of the two groups was the richer. The problem is not one of converting ducats into florins but of comparing information about income with information about property. A plausible estimate of the average wealth of a member of the Venetian élite in 1711 would be 150,000 ducats, which can be converted into 300,000 florins. For a comparable estimate of the wealth of the Amsterdam élite, it is necessary to go back to 1675. The average wealth of a member of the élite was then 167,000 florins, not much more than half the wealth of his Venetian opposite number — a surprising conclusion for the late seventeenth century, when Amsterdam was at its peak and Venice in decline.[46]

Other comparisons are both vaguer and simpler. Suppose we describe 'rentier' and 'entrepreneur' as contrasted psychological and economic types. Rentiers adopt a passive attitude to their wealth, entrepreneurs adopt an active attitude. By this definition, Venice seems to have been predominantly rentier (with some entrepreneurs) while Amsterdam was predominantly entrepreneur (with quite a few rentiers). In both places there was a shift from entrepreneur to rentier during the seventeenth century, a shift which will be the subject of a later chapter. With this major contrast other differences are associated. Land was an important investment in Venice but not in Amsterdam. Investment in joint-stock companies was important at Amsterdam but non-existent in Venice. Venice may have been colonialist in North Italy, but Venetians missed out on the much more profitable colonialism in the Indies.

In some Venetian cases, the profits of office were an important means of acquiring wealth. This source was relatively unimportant in Amsterdam, except perhaps in the case of the *schout*, or sheriff. About 1650 his official income was 500 florins, but his unofficial income was more like 6,000 florins.[47] In general the profits of politics were more indirect in Amsterdam. They consisted essentially of influencing the foreign policy of the Dutch Republic in the direction Amsterdam businessmen desired. To treat politics as a source of profit was natural in the seventeenth century, however it may shock the modern European. It may make comprehension of this fact, by no means confined to Venice and Amsterdam, somewhat easier if the reader remembers that politics was also a source of loss, that some men ruined themselves to live in the style demanded by the political offices they held. The style of life and the spending patterns of the two élites form the subject of the next chapter.

Style of Life

From the making and investing of wealth we now turn to the ways in which the two élites consumed it, and to the way of life which this spending made possible. Each of the two groups had, besides their distinctive attitudes and values (to be described in the next chapter) their own customary way of walking, talking, working, or relaxing, formed by training children to imitate a particular ideal.[1]

The Venetian style was the style of a nobility, who used coats of arms and were fascinated by genealogy. *Il Barbaro*, a compilation of the family trees of the whole Venetian nobility, was begun in the later sixteenth century. The proctors were a kind of higher nobility. They wore special purplish or bluish costumes which set them off from other nobles, with sleeves trailing the ground. They made a ceremonious entry to their new status after their election, with trumpets blowing, cannon firing, their portraits displayed in the streets; they distributed bread, wine and money to the people, and went in procession from the church of S. Salvador to the church of S. Marco.

In other ways the Venetians were, by European standards, a most unusual nobility. Their long black gowns made it clear that they belonged to the robe rather than the sword. Despite the fact that some of them had distinguished naval careers, they were essentially civilians. In general Venetian nobles did not wear swords in public. Like Chinese mandarins, whom they resembled in more than one way, Venetian nobles had traditionally bad seats on horses. In the fifteenth century the Florentine humanist, Poggio, recorded a joke about a Venetian who was unable to recognise his own horse, and in the early seventeenth century an English traveller, Coryat, noted: 'I saw but one horse in all Venice during the space of six weeks that I made my abode there.'[2]

Equally unusual for a nobility, the traditional Venetian style of life was one of frugality rather than display. Doge Lunardo Donà* is a good example to take, because in the early seventeenth century he was seen by contemporaries as a model Venetian nobleman. He was thrifty to the point of avarice. He told his heirs to live simply, and he bought his own carriage second-hand.[3] When Zuan Sagredo* was ambassador at Paris, so the contemporary story went, he would come back from audience with the king and tell his footmen to take off their liveries, to save wear and tear.[4] Coryat commented on the nobility in general that 'they keep no honourable hospitality, nor gallant retinue of servants about them, but a very frugal table', despite the wealth of some of them. He remarked on the fact that noblemen could be seen buying food in the markets themselves, which he thought beneath the dignity of their status.[5] This ideal was encouraged by sumptuary laws issued by the *provveditori alle pompe*, the 'overseers of displays'; sumptuary laws were common enough in seventeenth-century Europe, but these were applied to nobility. In 1658, for example, noble Venetians were forbidden to eat off silver plates and guests at banquets were forbidden to eat more than 1½ pounds of marzipan at a sitting.[6]

Gravity and dignity were also valued highly by Venetian nobles. Their robes forced them to walk in a slow and dignified manner and the use of the gondola made their progress that much more stately. Some members of the élite were conspicuous for their dignity. It was noted that Doge Francesco Morosini* would never cross his legs in public. Nicolò Corner* was described as having a 'fine presence' (*bellissima presenza*) and a royal manner. This cultural style was formed by imitating the old men, for the doge and the proctors usually were old men. Of the 25 doges elected between 1578 and 1720, the average age at election was 67. Fynes Morison, who visited Venice in 1594, made the perceptive comment that Venetians seem old early, 'and rather seem than truly be aged'.[7] Where else but Venice could they call the group led by Donà* the 'youngsters' (*giovani*)? Donà was 46 in 1582 and 70 when he was elected doge. Ceremoniousness was also part of the Venetian style. Coryat noticed that Venetian nobles 'give a low congie to each other by very civil and courteous gestures, as by bending of their bodies and clapping their right hand upon their breasts'. Another visitor commented on their habit of kissing a man's sleeve as a greeting.[8]

Another ingredient of the Venetian cultural style was silence. The late-sixteenth-century allegorical paintings in the Doge's Palace included not only 'fame' and 'victory' but also 'taciturnity'. Lunardo Donà* wrote a note to himself, 'don't be loquacious' (*non esser loquace*).[9] A studied inscrutability was the ideal. 'One never knows whether he loves or hates anything', wrote Sarpi about Donà.* It was not only at Carnival that Venetians wore masks. Their interest in simulation and dissimulation may owe something to their daily

visits to the *broglio* (p. 68 below). Antonio Colluraffi, a private tutor
to some Venetian nobles, advised nobles at the *broglio* to penetrate
the thoughts of others 'in order to accommodate oneself the better
to their humours' (*per potessi a'loro humori più agevolmente
conformare*). Antonio Ottobon,* in his advice to his son, recommended him to model himself on Proteus and please everyone by
being all things to all men. (*Tu dovrai qual Proteo mutar figure per
renderti grato ad ognuno.*) A more hostile observer suggested that
Venetian noblemen 'dissimulate a great deal among themselves,
and however greatly they might hate someone, they always put on
a friendly face'.[10] If contemporaries found them difficult to under-
stand, the twentieth-century historian of the Venetian nobility had
better beware.

The noble Venetian style of life, then, was marked by frugality,
by gravity and by prudence. Its dominant note was self-control. The
ethos discouraged eating, drinking, talking and spending money in
excess of requirements. Lunardo Donà* added to this a vow of chastity,
and of Nicolò Contarini* it was said that he died a virgin. The individual was expected to suppress his own desires for the sake of his
house or for the sake of Venice. 'I should like to be known in
the Roman curia as ambassador of Venice . . . and not as Lunardo Donà;
and equally in Venice as senator of that fatherland . . . and not by my
private name.' Donà* asked his heirs to spend only 500 ducats on his
monument. Whether modesty or avarice, it extended beyond the grave.
A number of the élite declare in their wills that they want to be buried
without any pomp (unusual for a seventeenth-century noble) and
Ferigo Contarini* went so far as to enforce his wishes under penalty
of losing 10,000 ducats.[11]

This style of life, and probably its gravity and ceremoniousness
in particular, struck one seventeenth-century observer as a 'Spanish'
style. But during the century a rival 'French' style came to emerge:
more open, more flamboyant, more generous, more relaxed. Nicolò
Corner* was described as friendly and even 'jovial'; Piero Dolfin*
was gay, pleasant and full of promises which he did not keep;
Francesco Contarini* had a 'gentle manner' (*dolce maniera*); doge
Domenico Contarini* impressed a French visitor by his *douceur* and
his *affabilité*.[12] Even horse-riding was becoming more popular among
young noblemen in the period. A joust was organized at Padua in
1600 by the *podestà* and the *capitano*, and from the mid seventeenth
century on there was a riding-school in Venice, La Cavallerizza, at

the Mendicanti. Finally, though it is difficult to measure this, one has the impression that conspicuous consumption was increasing.[13]

Among Venetian nobles, an ideal of personal frugality coexisted with an emphasis on public splendour, for the honour of the family or the honour of the state, *il publico decoro*, as Francesco Erizzo described it.[14] Domenico Contarini* referred in his will to the 'luxury' necessary to keep up the style of a doge (*sostener si gran grado*). There is evidence of this stress on public splendour no matter what the expense throughout the period. When Henri III visited Venice in 1574 he was entertained magnificently by Ferigo Contarini* in his villa at Mira on the Brenta; and when the minor German prince Ernst August visited Venice in 1685, he was entertained magnificently by Marco Contarini* in his villa at Piazzola; his host even laid on a mock naval battle in the villa grounds.[15] To hold high office involved great expense. Marin Grimani* spent 6,943 ducats on the celebrations when he was elected doge in 1595 (it was characteristic of a Venetian nobleman to record his expenses so precisely).[16] To serve as a *rettore* on the mainland might be costly. Andrea Contarini* refers in his will to the 'enormous expense' involved when he was *rettore* at Udine. Contemporaries remarked on the 'splendour' with which Zuanbattista Corner* served as *provveditore* of Peschiera and *capitano* of Bergamo in the 1640s.[17] Another expensive office was *Capitan Generale da Mar.* Most expensive of all, in all probability, was the office of ambassador. It was not unknown for a man's enemies to intrigue to have him appointed ambassador in order to ruin him.[18] Nicolò Corner* was said to have spent 20,000 ducats in a few days on an extraordinary embassy to the Emperor. This figure should not be taken too seriously. For one extraordinary embassy to the Emperor, undertaken by Anzolo Contarini* and Renier Zen,* an itemized expense account has survived.[19] The journey there and back cost them 2,500 ducats. This included the cost of transporting and feeding their retinue, plus incidental expenses like tips to trumpeters, alms to churches on the route and the painting of shields to leave behind at the inns where they stayed. All the same, 2,500 ducats was a lot to spend in a few days, and an ordinary ambassador held his post for about three years. It is no wonder that at the end of the seventeenth century it was sometimes difficult to find nobles who would accept the appointment. Alvise Pisani* was appointed ambassador to France in 1698 after four previous candidates had refused. Being a Pisani of S. Stefano, he could afford it.

The Amsterdam élite had no such conscious traditional style, perhaps because they belonged not to an estate but to a class, not to a formally defined group but to something more informal. It is true that some of them were knighted, as a result of missions abroad: Reynier Pauw* was knighted by both James I and Louis XIII, Dirck Bas* by Gustav Adolf, Willem Backer* became a knight of S. Marco at Venice in 1647. Some members of the élite bought country estates with titles attached. Jacob de Graeff* became *Vrijheer* of Zuid-Polsbroek after buying this estate from the prince of Aremberg in 1610; Cornelis Bicker* became *Heer* of Swieten after buying the estate of Swieten, near Leyden, in 1632; Joan Huydecoper* became *Heer* of Marsseveen after buying that estate in 1640. A few members of the élite can already be found in the early seventeenth century compiling family trees and trying to prove noble descent. Gerard Schaep* scoffed at another patrician for 'the vainglory of his family tree' (*die ydele glorie van sijn geslachtboom*) but his papers survive to show that he believed his own family descended from the Silesian nobility.[20] Andries de Graeff* claimed descent from the von Graben, a noble family from the Tyrol. However, this group within the élite (probably a small minority) was not formally distinct from the rest. No one could have listed the patricians of Amsterdam in the way that the golden book listed the patricians of Venice. The Amsterdam élite wore no official robes like the doge, proctors or senators of Venice. On official occasions they wore the same black gowns or coats as professional men and businessmen usually wore. Their movements were not particularly ceremonious. Although they lived on canals they did not glide in gondolas, but walked the streets like everyone else. The British ambassador, Henry Sidney, remarked with surprise that burgomaster Gillis Valckenier* 'walks about without a footman': 'He walks about the street just like an ordinary shopkeeper.' Another British ambassador, Sir William Temple, generalised the point when he wrote that the burgomasters of Amsterdam 'are obliged to no sort of expense, more than ordinary modest citizens, in their habits, their attendance, their tables'. On the contrary, they 'appear in all places with the simplicity and modesty of other private citizens'.[21] This point struck the Venetians too. Tommaso Contarini, visiting the Dutch Republic in 1610, was struck by the simple style of life there, which he thought the Venetians had not even paralled in the time of their ancestors.[22]

The Amsterdam style does seem to have become somewhat grander during the period. Nicolaes Tulp* attacked sumptuous wedding feasts and had a law against them passed in 1655. This did not stop Louys Trip* from spending 8,300 florins on the wedding of his daughter Anna Maria to Wouter Valckenier* in 1670 (money well spent, for this alliance helped him enter the Town Council in 1672). In the eighteenth century these changes went still further. They can be illustrated from the tax-assessments of 1742, when information was collected about such status symbols as country houses, coaches and horses. Country houses grew bigger in the eighteenth century and imitated the French more. Costume also symbolised an important change in the style of life of the Dutch regents as a whole. In the seventeenth century they wore sober black; in the eighteenth century they had themselves painted in coloured clothes. Self-control was less of a virtue than before.

Of course there were variations within the two groups as well as differences between them. The Venetians included a bluff sea-dog like Francesco Molin,* known for his hard drinking and his rough direct way of speaking, they also included Pietro Basadonna,* 'a cunning, polished courtier' (*scaltro e raffinato cortigiano*), who was always smiling in his sardonic way.[23] Differences like these were not just differences between individual temperaments, but differences of cultural style associated with differences in social role. The Venetian élite, which monopolized power in the whole state, needed naval officers like Molin* and diplomats like Basadonna.* In Amsterdam there was less spectacular variety because there was less need for variety. Amsterdammers were in the main a group of merchants, and the bulk of Dutch diplomats and naval officers came from elsewhere. C.P. Hooft* and Reynier Pauw* differed very greatly in attitudes, but not very much in life-style.

Like the French *noblesse de robe* but unlike most European nobilities of the seventeenth century, the élites of both Amsterdam and Venice were essentially urban groups.

In Venice the main residence of each branch of the clan was the palace in town, not the villa or villas on the mainland. The branch might take its name from the part of Venice in which the palace was situated, like the Foscarini *ai carmini*, in the parish of the Carmelite church, or the Grimani *ai servi*, in the parish of the Servites. It was the town palace on which most money was spent, and the town palace where the branch spent most of the year. The élite had to stay in town. In the first place, they had to do so for political reasons. The state

was governed from the doge's palace, where the Greater Council
met, and the Senate, and the College, and the Council of Ten. The
doge could not leave Venice without permission. Other nobles could
leave when they wanted, but the Senate usually met every Saturday
(much more often in times of crisis) and the Greater Council every
Sunday morning. Of course a council with some two thousand members could not do all its business in one morning a week; hence the
crucial importance of another urban institution, the *broglio.* Foreign
visitors noticed that Piazza S. Marco and its piazzetta were full of
nobles 'in great troops' every day between five and eight in the evening.
It was here that the higher nobility paid court to the lower, soliciting
their votes for the following Sunday. A political market-place, as
more then one visitor remarked, but everything done with great
ceremony and deep bows. If a noble did not bow low enough, he was
said to be 'stiff-backed' (*duro di schiena*) and had trouble getting what
he wanted. It is thanks to Venice that *broglio,* in modern Italian, has
changed its meaning from 'garden' to 'intrigue'.[24] Piazza S. Marco
was an important part of the 'front' for the self-presentation of the
Venetian nobles. It was the stage on which they acted, with the
common people and the foreign visitors as the spectators. On this
stage they learned the arts of simulation and dissimulation. The
historian can only regret that Pietro Malombra's painting of the
broglio has been lost.[25]

It was in town that two important leisure institutions of the nobility
were located: the gambling saloon (*ridotto*) and the academy. In the
sixteenth century, gambling had taken the form of bets on elections
to the Greater Council. This was forbidden by the government, and
in the seventeenth century gambling took the politically more
innocuous form of playing cards for money in public rooms provided
for the purpose. Among the enthusiasts were Bertucci Valier,*
Daniele IV Dolfin,* Silvestro Valier* and Giacomo Correr,* who
spent his winnings paying his fines for refusing political office. No
doubt their studied inscrutability was an asset to patrician gamblers.

As for the academy, by the seventeenth century it was not so much
an informal group of friends as a club, with a fixed meeting-place,
'protectors' and a 'device' (*impresa*). It was organised by nobles,
though commoners might be invited to join. The Delphic Academy,
for example, met in the palace of senator Francesco Gussoni; its protectors were Zuanbattista Corner* and Alvise Duodo;* its device
was a tripod, with the motto 'from here the oracle' (*hinc oracula*).

Cristoforo Ivanovitch, a well-known poetaster of the period, was one of the commoners who were members.[26] Two of the best-known academies of the period were the 'Huntress' (*Cacciatrice*), and the 'Unknown Ones' (*Incogniti*). The *Cacciatrice* met in the palace of senator Andrea Morosini. Giordano Bruno expounded his views there. Members included Nicolò Contarini,* Lunardo Donà* and, among the commoners, Paolo Sarpi, the famous Servite friar, polymath and historian of the Council of Trent. It was a convention that during meetings members 'did not stand on ceremony' with one another.[27] The *Incogniti* were founded by Zuanfrancesco Loredan and met in his palace. Its members quite literally came incognito: they wore masks. This at once solved the problem of ceremony in a mixed gathering of nobles and commoners, and made it possible to express unorthodox religious views without fear of the consequences—there were informers and inquisitors in seventeenth-century Venice. One member of the *Incogniti* was the famous 'libertine' Ferrante Pallavicino, and women were allowed to attend their meetings, which had an erotic, frivolous yet learned atmosphere not unlike that of a Paris salon of the period. The members discussed such topics as the value of ugliness, why A is the first letter of the alphabet, and why Pythagoras objected to beans.[28] Two more good reasons for the Venetian nobility to stay in town in autumn and winter were the opera and the carnival.

Despite this emphasis on the city *villeggiatura*—to repair to one's country villa—was a well-known Venetian practice. The most popular place to have a villa was along the Brenta; many of the villas, more or less dilapidated, are still there today. Villas were farms—the importance of land to the Venetian élite has already been discussed—but they were also holiday residences. Thus Domenico Contarini* referred to a visit to his villa at Valnogaredo 'to take a little relaxation in those hills of ours', and Agostino Nani* built a villa at Monselice with an entrance arch over which was the following inscription: 'You are off duty here; take off your robes' (*Emeritam hic, suspende togam*).[29] The 'ebb and flow' of the nobles along the Brenta was an event as regular as the tides. The summer season began on 12 June and ended with the end of July. The autumn season began on 4 October and ended in mid November. For its owner and his friends the villa was a refuge from city life, a means of escape from plague, from summer heat and from politics. In it he could study or drive away the almost inevitable boredom with chess or cards, parlour games or practical jokes.[30] Near the villa he could shoot hares or go fowling in a boat with a bow and pellets of terracotta. Even when he hunted, the Venetian nobleman did not mount a horse.[31]

Amsterdam patricians were still more of an urban group than Venetian ones. They tended to congregate along a few canals; the most popular, for members of the élite, were the Herengracht, and the Keizersgracht, which look today much as they did in 1700. For political reasons they needed to be within easy reach of the Town Hall, where the burgomasters, councillors and magistrates all had their chambers. There was no *broglio* in Amsterdam, no Greater Council to court, no need to formalise the process of intrigue and bargaining. The élite also needed to stay in town to be within easy reach of the Bourse, East India House, West India House and the harbour itself. This was why to be sent no further than The Hague was exile for an Amsterdam patrician.

However, the Amsterdam élite were not entirely urban either. They too had their country estates and their villas, or shares in villas (at least a third of the group); farms (*hofsteden*), country places (*buitenplaatsen*), pleasure-houses (*lusthuizen*) or play-houses (*speelhuizen*) they called them. This aspect of their lives seems not to have attracted the attention it deserves, nor have the villas themselves, most of which have disappeared.[32] As the names 'pleasure-house' and 'play-house' suggest, these villas were places for recreation as well as investments; we have seen that land was not an important investment for the élite in the latter part of the period, when references to villas are most numerous. The names of some of the individual houses confirm this impression that their use was for relaxation; *Buitensorg* (Sans Souci), *Tijdverdrijf* (Pass the Time) and *Vredenhof* (Peace-Haven) are among them.[33] The favourite sites for these villas were along the Amstel and along the Vecht, from Muiden to Utrecht. This area was a bourgeois Arcadia, evoked in romances like Heemskerk's *Batavian Arcadia* and Zesen's *Adriatic Rosamond*, which describes a Venetian nobleman living with his daughters in a villa on the Amstel; or in the engravings of *The triumphant Vecht*, published in 1719, which parallel the Venetian villas illustrated at the same time by Coronelli.[34] At the end of the seventeenth century one finds the Town Council meeting relatively rarely, if at all, in June and August. It is likely that its members had disappeared to their pleasure-houses.[35] However, it should be emphasized that what these houses offered, like Venetian villas, was a temporary escape, and not a permanent alternative to urban life. In this respect they resemble their democratic equivalents for the Amsterdammers of today, the chalets and allotments at Sloterdijk.

Attitudes and Values

Compared with the other noblemen of seventeenth-century Europe, the Venetians had another peculiarity which has not yet been mentioned: they liked writing books. The Venetian nobility as a whole published more than a hundred books between 1580 and 1658; the most popular categories were poems; plays; orations; philosophy; and history, in that order.[1] The books published by members of the élite include Nicolò Contarini's* *The Perfection of the Universe*, a general survey which makes him the one member of the group to offer an explicit world-view; Paolo Paruta's* *Perfection of Political Life* (his *Discourses* and his *History of Venice* were published after his death); Battista Nani's* *History of Venice*; Zuan Sagredo's* romance, *Arcadia on the Brenta*, written when he was young and published under an anagrammatic pseudonym, and his *History of the Ottoman Empire*, written when he was mature and published under his own name; and Nicolò da Ponte's treatise on geometry, said to have been published in the year of his death.[2]

The unpublished treatises by members of the élite form an almost equally important collection. They include the poems of Simone Contarini* and of Antonio Ottobon,* the latter in dialect; Daniele IV Dolfin's* treatise on the art of war; Paolo Tiepolo's* history of Cyprus; and, most famous of all, Nicolò Contarini's* history of Venice, which had a considerable circulation in manuscript.[3] This last book remained unpublished for political reasons. A working party advised the Council of Ten that the book contained maxims of state which were better kept secret than divulged.[4] This fact that the others were not published suggests the Venetian emphasis on the role of the cultivated amateur.

Seventeenth-century nobles who published books often liked to protest that they were not professional writers (still a low-status group in this period) but in Venice the idea of the amateur seems even more important than elsewhere. As we have seen, it affected their political system too. The amateur ideal is expressed most explicitly in Antonio Colluraffi's *The Venetian noble* (1623), a treatise on their education by a professional tutor. Given this background, it may not be anachronistic to give the term *dilettante* (used of a Venetian nobleman in Boschini's dialogue on painting) its modern sense rather than the literal meaning of one who delights in something.[5] One Venetian nobleman who dabbled in literature declared, 'I am a Venetian gentleman and I have never hoped to be known as a literary man.'[6] One suspects irony behind that 'hoped'. Zuan Sagredo* described the noble heroes of his *Arcadia on the Brenta* as 'well-informed but not academic, carrying their learning lightly' (*dotti senza professione, eruditi senza ostentatione*).[7] Zuanfrancesco Loredan, sometime councillor of Ten and the leading literary figure of mid-century Venice, was said to devote his days to politics and to write his stories only at night.[8] Battista Nani's* history of Venice gave one contemporary the impression that it had been written in haste by a man preoccupied with other matters.[9] Nani* was in fact an extremely active diplomat, who was elected ambassador seven times. Perhaps the unpolished impression given by his history was a deliberate one, an example of what Castiglione called *sprezzatura*, the affectation of effortlessness. Nani* was famous for having the ear of the house: 'When he speaks in the Senate, the whole place is hushed.'[10] But the Senate did not like polish; it preferred 'Attic' prose to 'Asiatic', a plain or 'senatorial' speech to an ornate or 'academic' one.[11] In short, the Venetians tended to have a pragmatic cast of mind and to prefer figures of arithmetic to figures of rhetoric. This tendency can be documented from the *relazioni*, or reports which returning diplomats and administrators of the mainland had to read out in public. They are cool in tone and full of precise facts and figures.

These reports are also good evidence of Venetian interest in history, since they regularly explain the situation in France, say, or in the Ottoman Empire by making reference to the past. Another sign of the élite's interest in history is the fact that the Venetian government regularly appointed official historians. The histories of Paruta,* Contarini* and Nani* were all commissioned in this way.[12] This interest in history was a pragmatic one. History should be written, Nicolò Contarini* remarked, not to exhibit eloquence but to help in political affairs. The historian could help, so it was often thought in the seventeenth century, by formulating political maxims and illustrating them with examples, so that the reader could extract political observations for meditation, as Lunardo Donà* did when he was reading Guicciardini's *History of Italy*.[13] Venetian official history was of course among other things an instrument of propaganda, the literary equivalent of the historical paintings in the doge's palace. But interest in the past was not entirely utilitarian. The library of Ferigo Contarini* included forty-five books on Roman antiquities, on coins, medals, inscriptions, statues, triumphs, families, religion and military discipline.[14] Venetian nobles liked to identify themselves with Romans.[15] Think of their predilection for such terms as 'senate', 'toga', or 'patrician'. The Corner clan (and the Venetian clan was not so unlike the Roman *gens*) claimed descent from the Roman Cornelii, the Loredan from Mutius Scaevola, and the Zustinian from the emperor Justinian.

There is much less evidence of patrician interest in the natural sciences ('natural philosophy' was the term used at the time) although such an interest did exist. The best-known example is that of Zuanfrancesco Sagredo, not a member of the élite but a close relative of some of them. He was friendly with Galileo, who put him into two dialogues; was interested in astronomy and magnetism, had his own workshop and made scientific instruments himself.[16] Another important example is Nicolò Contarini,* whose *The Perfection of the Universe* discusses (besides God and the angels) the elements and the planets. He encouraged the medical researches of Dr Santorio Santorio, was interested in hydraulics, and had 'a large machine' constructed in his garden to raise water.[17] He and Lunardo Donà* were regular visitors to the Accademia Cacciatrice, where discussions on the natural sciences took place, and Donà* was friendly with Galileo. Battista Nani* and other members of his academy, 'The Truth-lovers' (*Filaleti*) were interested in botany, and Zuanbattista Corner* owned 'mathematical and geometrical instruments'.[18]

These examples must not be given too much emphasis. The Cacciatrice was equally concerned with questions of theology and ethics, and in general it may be argued that the Venetian ethos of the aristocratic amateur was a discouragment to scientific research. It allowed only two attitudes to the natural sciences. The first was a collector's interest. Ferigo Contarini* had a typical undiscriminating *Wunderkammer* of the years around 1600 which included minerals and bones, a cat's testicles and a buffalo's horn.[19] The second possible attitude to the natural sciences was the utilitarian attitude of a governing élite. When Galileo was a professor at Padua, Antonio Priuli* went up the tower of S. Marco 'to see the marvels and singular effects of the telescope of the said Galileo', but then a telescope had practical value for a naval power.[20] Besides Nicolò Contarini,* Pola Antonio Belegno* and Anzolo Diedo* were interested in machines. Belegno* had 'a hydraulic machine' constructed to serve his palace and its garden. This pragmatic or utilitarian attitude is summed up in Colluraffi's treatise on education, which recommends the Venetian noble student to leave 'subtle and over-curious investigations', to others, and to study mathematics only in so far as it is relevant to 'the interests of the commonwealth.'[21] Mathematics was associated with military studies in a Paduan academy for Venetian nobles, the *Delia,* founded by Pietro Duodo when he was *capitano* of Padua in 1607, believing as he did that the 'mathematical sciences' were necessary knowledge for 'a perfect gentleman and soldier' (*perfetto cavaliere e soldato*). The *Delia* later on had Zuan Pesaro* as its 'protector'.[22]

This brief sketch of the interests of Venetian nobles confirms the current emphasis on the pragmatic, empirical nature of the Venetian style of thought. But it would not do to forget that it was also deeply marked by scholasticism, especially the local variety, the Aristotelianism of the 'school of Padua'. Nicolò Contarini's* book on the perfection of the universe discusses the opinions of Aquinas, Ockham and Gregory of Rimini. Lunardo Donà* was particularly interested in the philosophy of Aquinas. Descartes seems to have made little impact on seventeenth-century Venice, though his ideas and those of Malebranche are discussed by the philosopher Bernardo Trevisan. In 1600 Venetians had been abreast of new ideas, but in 1700 this was no longer the case. Tradition was powerful and the propensity to innovate was weak. Perhaps this was the price of their notable past achievements. This conservatism may (as Addison thought) have contributed to Venetian economic decline, for 'a trading nation must be still for new changes, and expedients as different junctures and emergencies arise.'[23]

The Amsterdam élite also published books, but they give a rather different impression. Their publications include a book on magnetism by Laurens Reael;* the observations on medicine of Nicolaes Tulp;* the treatises on botany of Joan Commelin;* the atlases of the publisher Joan Blaeu;* a tragedy, *Medea,* by Jan Six;* the religious outpourings of Coenraad van Beuningen;* Johannes Hudde's* letters on algebra and geometry; and, best-known of all, two books by Nicolaes Witsen,* one on ship-building and one on North and East Tartary.[24] This list suggests a much greater interest in the natural sciences than there was in Venice; and one should add to it the fact that two of the élite,

P.J. Hooft* and Jacob de Graeff,* shared a laboratory and were supposed to have found the *perpetuum mobile.* P. J. Hooft* studied medicine and chemistry.

The list also suggests that the Amsterdam patricians took rather less interest in history than the Venetians, but this point needs qualification. One of the most distinguished historians in seventeenth-century Europe, P.C. Hooft, 'the Dutch Tacitus', was the son of a burgomaster of Amsterdam, and his father, C.P. Hooft* was not ignorant of history either. C.P. Hooft's* papers refer to sixteen historical works which include Livy, Josephus, Guicciardini, Sleidan (the *Commentaries* on sixteenth-century German political and ecclesiastical affairs), Foxe, Camden (the *Annals*) and the Dutch historian Bor.[25] His still more learned colleague, burgomaster Martin Coster,* owned copies of Herodotus, Thucydides, Xenophon, Livy, Plutarch and Josephus, to mention only ancient historians. Among the moderns, he had books by the Italian humanist Flavio Biondo, the chronicle of the German Sebastian Franck, the memoirs of Philippe de Commynes, and the history of his own time by the Italian bishop Paolo Giovio; he had the history of France by Paolo Emilio; the history of Poland by Martin Cromer; the history of England by Polidore Vergil; and the history of Florence by Machiavelli.[26] If there was any 'Renaissance man' among the Amsterdam elite it was surely Coster,* who had studied in Italy in the mid sixteenth century. It is also true that Amsterdam, like Venice, had an official historian at one point, the Lombard Gregorio Leti, appointed in 1689.[27]

This interest in history was in part a utilitarian one. P.C. Hooft, dedicating his biography of Henri IV of France to Dirck Bas,* discussed the special value of history to rulers. C.P. Hooft* regularly argued from historical precedent in the Town Council. He quoted the fact that Moses was above Aaron as an 'example' which proves that the preachers of Amsterdam should not tell the Council what to do. There was also a good measure of identification with the past. The Dutch preoccupation with the Batavian revolt against Rome is well known; it was expressed in plays by P.C. Hooft and Vondel and in paintings by Rembrandt and Govert Flinck for the Amsterdam Town Hall.[28] The Dutch identified themselves with their ancestors the Batavians and the Spanish empire with the Roman. But they could not resist seeing themselves as Romans on occasion. In a pamphlet called *Fin de la guerre*, published at Amsterdam in the early seventeenth century, Scipio Africanus and Fabius Maximus talk about the best way to attack Carthage, and the dialogue slides into the argument that Spain should be attacked in her most vulnerable spot, the West Indies.[29]   The books and funeral monuments of members of the Amsterdam élite often carry Latin inscriptions referring to them as *consul* (if burgomaster) or *senator* (if a member of the Town Council), and they might refer to Scipio or Fabius Maximus as 'burgomasters' of Rome. The Amsterdam élite, as one might have expected from a largely Calvinist group, also identified with Old Testament figures such as Solomon and Moses. In the Town Hall, the councillor's chamber contained one painting of Solomon praying for wisdom and one of Moses advised by Jethro; the magistrate's chamber contained a painting of Moses and the Tables of the Law.[30]

History was also studied for its own sake. This is revealed most clearly in the writings of Nicolaes Witsen,* who was an enthusiastic antiquarian. He was interested in the design of triremes, in the ships represented in Egyptian hieroglyphics and on medieval seals, in an ancient mirror found in Siberia, in the authenticity of Dr Woodward's Roman shield.[31]   He was also fascinated by the diversity of languages and customs.

The idea that history is a storehouse of political examples was of course common enough in seventeenth-century Europe. What is much less common is to find a ruling group so interested in the natural sciences. One obvious reason for this was the presence of professional doctors on the town council, something without an equivalent in Venice. Nicolaes Tulp's* scientific learning sprang from his medical studies. Another reason for interest in the natural sciences was something shared with Venice, the involvement of the élite with the sea. This may explain why Admiral Dr Laurens Reael* should have written on magnetism, and why Willem Blaeu, sometime pupil of the great Danish astronomer Tyge Brahe, should have decided to come to Amsterdam to make globes and maps, passing his geographical interests on to his son Joan Blaeu.* Disinterested curiosity seems predominant in Nicolaes Witsen,* in his scientific studies as in his historical ones. He was interested in mammoths and in comets and in whether a so-called unicorn's horn really belonged to a narwhal. He was a fellow of the Royal Society, and corresponded with its members about unusual shells and the question of whether Nova Zembla was a continent.[32]   Disinterested curiosity also seems predominant in Joannes Hudde,* who was said to be one of the best mathematicians of his day, was interested in astronomy, optics and medicine, and was on friendly terms with Huygens, Leibniz and Spinoza. He abandoned his studies for a political career, but retained an interest in hydraulics and was in charge of the technical side of operations when the dykes were broken in 1672 as a last defence against the French invaders.[33]

One may suspect that the social background of Witsen* and Hudde* was relevant to their interests. In his book on ship-building, Witsen* betrayed a fascination with technical details, such as the exact measurements of planks, which in other parts of Europe might have been thought beneath a gentleman. He even drew some of the illustrations himself, just as he had once made etchings to illustrate Ovid's *Metamorphoses.* Hudde* clearly had no inhibitions about the pursuit of such 'subtle and over-curious investigations' as mathematics. Perhaps Witsen* and Hudde* were able to indulge their interests because they did not identify with noble values.

Novelty, that entrepreneurial virtue, seems to have been accepted more easily in seventeenth-century Amsterdam than in Venice, or indeed most parts of Europe in the period. As C.P. Hooft* put it, 'not all novelty is bad and not all antiquity is good'. His defence of novelty was to quote instances of valuable new discoveries in astronomy, medicine and navigation; an interest in innovation and an interest in the natural sciences went naturally together.[34] An interest in novelty is expressed in two inaugural lectures at the Amsterdam Athenaeum, where a number of the élite were educated. Professor Blasius lectured in 1659 on *New discoveries (De rebus noviter inventis)*, discussing Harvey and the circulation of the blood; and Professor de Raey lectured in 1669 on *The wisdom of the ancients (De sapientia veterum)*, suggesting that some ancient 'wisdom' was not wisdom at all.[35]

The style of thought of C.P. Hooft* has been characterized as empiricist, rationalist and individualist.[36] In the course of the seventeenth century one can observe the penetration, in patrician circles, of a consciously mathematical style of thought which owes not a little to Descartes and to Spinoza. An example of the application of the geometrical method to political decision-making can be found among the papers of Joannes Hudde.* He is commenting on a project of defensive alliance with France. He begins with a definition of a 'defensive alliance', then states an axiom, that the chief aim of all individuals and states is their own conservation, and concludes that the idea of a defensive alliance with an enemy is absurd.[37]

These examples may tempt the historian to exaggerate the modernity of the Amsterdam élite, their combination of rationalism,

Protestantism, capitalism and science. As a corrective, it might be valuable to look at the case of Coenraed van Beuningen.* Van Beuningen* is best known as a highly-skilled negotiator, but he was also a man of wide interests, including literature, history and the natural sciences. He was friendly with the biologist Jan Swammerdam, and interested in the ideas of Descartes. He combined all this with an interest in mysticism, millennarianism, astrology, dream interpretation, and 'supernatural wonders'. Van Beuningen* may well have been a schizoid type. He suffered a breakdown in 1688, and went round the streets preaching about the end of the world; he was placed under guardianship. However, to dismiss his non-rational interests as nothing but a form of madness would be a superficial interpretation. Many sane people in the seventeenth century shared these interests. Van Beuningen* is an interesting but not an isolated example of the coexistence of new science, Cartesianism, astrology, and millennarianism inside one man's head. [38]

The religious attitudes of the patricians of Venice and Amsterdam were more alike than one might have expected, given that one city was officially Catholic and the other predominantly Protestant. In Venice 'Catholic' and 'Papist' were not the same, observed the French ambassador even before the Interdict. After the pope had laid Venice under interdict in 1606, the Venetian case was presented by the Republic's official theologian, Paolo Sarpi. In Sarpi's writings the difference between 'Catholic' and 'Papist' is clear enough. Sarpi believed that the primitive church (representing the true 'Catholic' position), had been democratic, poor, unworldly and austere, while the contemporary ('Papist') church was monarchical, rich, worldly and corrupt; that the great obstacle to the necessary reform of the church was the triple alliance of the pope, Spain and the Jesuits; that the Augustinian emphasis on man's need for grace was nearer the truth than the Jesuit emphasis on free will.[39]

Was Sarpi's view the view of the Venetian élite? A similar cluster of attitudes can certainly be found in Nicolò Contarini,* a man of austere morality who wanted the church to keep out of temporal affairs and hated the Jesuits for their use of religion as a political tool. Augustinian on the question of grace, he followed the Calvinist Synod of Dort (Dordrecht) in the Netherlands, with interest, and his sympathies were not with the Arminians (sometimes accused of being

Catholics in disguise) but with the Gomarists (see p. 81 below).[40] His was an interior religion; his will makes an unusually brief mention of the Virgin and the saints. Some of these attitudes can be found among other patricians of the period. Lunardo Donà* was equally anti-Spanish and critical of the papacy, though he was not opposed to Counter-Reformation spirituality. He read the devotional writings of S. Carlo Borromeo and Fray Luis de Granada, noting that the latter should be 'read twice a year'.[41] Antonio Priuli,* according to his will, hoped to reach heaven 'thanks only to the blood shed for us by Our Lord Jesus Christ'. Nicolò da Ponte* was interested in St Augustine, and defended the Venetian heretic Buccella; his brother Andrea fled to Calvin's Geneva; pope Pius V thought him a bad Catholic, though the patriarch of Jerusalem thought him a good one.[42] The reports of some patricians who had served as ambassadors to Rome show that they were anti-Spanish and hostile to the pope for supporting Spain; examples which spring to mind are Polo Tiepolo,* Polo Paruta,* Agostino Nani* and Simone Contarini.* One might describe this group, which overlaps if it does not coincide with the faction of the 'youngsters' in Venetian politics, as anti-papal, in the sense of opposing the jurisdictional claims of the pope, and anti-clerical, at least in the sense of opposing clerical exemption from lay justice and lay taxation. There is some evidence, from members of the nobility, but not from members of the élite, of more radical unorthodoxy. Zuanfrancesco Loredan and his circle are the most famous examples of what the seventeenth century called 'libertines'.[43]

However, it would be misleading not to point to equally outstanding examples of an opposed religious attitude. On these issues the élite were not cohesive. There was a devout party, or, if 'party' is too strong a term, a faction or a group of patricians who were more favourably disposed towards the papacy. Papal families were regularly made honorary Venetian nobles; the Aldobrandini, the Peretti, even the Borghese, the family of Pope Paul V, who laid Venice under interdict. The more prominent members of the devout faction included Zuanne Dolfin,* who ended his life as a cardinal; it was said that he was elected proctor as a reward for bringing some important relics to Venice.[44] They included Marin Grimani,* who was knighted by Pope Sixtus V and left money for masses to be said by the Jesuits; Ferigo Contarini,* described by the nuncio at Venice in 1593 as 'always favourable to the church'; Giacomo Foscarini,* who wanted to have the Jesuit college at Padua reopened. They included Zuan I Corner,* described by the

Spanish ambassador as 'fearful of God', whose son was a cardinal, and to whom was dedicated a treatise on Venetian relics written by the noble priest Zuan Tiepolo.[46] Zuan Pesaro* was another supporter of the Jesuits.

If one looks at the wills made by members of the élite over the whole period, it is to find, in the majority of cases, considerable emphasis on the outward forms of religion which make the testaments of Nicolo Contarini* and Antonio Priuli* seem exceptional. The proctors ask to be buried in the habit of a Franciscan or a Capuchin; they leave money for three hundred, five hundred, or even three thousand masses; they express their devotion to patron saints and (a relatively new cult this) to guardian angels; Zuan Bembo* once offered a silver ship to the Holy House of Loreto; Zuan I Corner* asked for someone to make a pilgrimage there in his name; Alvise Barbarigo* kept the relics of S. Sulpicio in his villa.[47]

Individual examples like this are of course a poor substitute for a questionnaire. The nearest approach to a questionnaire on this subject we owe to the Jesuits, who made a survey in 1620 about the attitude of senators to the readmission of the Society to Venice. They estimated that at least half the senators were opposed. The fact that Venice opposed the pope up to the point of interdict and beyond in 1606 suggests that the majority of the ruling élite at this point supported an anti-papal policy in the sense that they saw the pope as acting merely as a temporal prince when he attacked the 'liberties' or privileges of Venice. Yet the wills of the élite suggest that most of them accepted an exterior religion, an impression confirmed by such a collective act of devotion as the building of the church of the *Salute* by order of the Senate as 'an appropriate means to placate the wrath of heaven'.[48]   How is one to reconcile the apparent contradiction? It looks as if what happened in 1606 was that at a time when Venice seemed threatened by Spain and the pope was a friend of Spain, the silent majority of patricians was prepared to accept the leadership of a hardline anti-papal group whose other religious attitudes they did not share.

Curiously enough, this was exactly the situation in some Dutch towns during the revolt of the Netherlands. The fear of Spain persuaded the silent majority to accept the leadership of a minority of Calvinists. In Amsterdam in 1578, a group of former religious exiles took over the city government. They included Wilhelm Baerdesen,* Reynier Cant* (a leading Calvinist who had been living in Bremen), Martin Coster,* Adriaen Cromhout* (another leading Calvinist who had been living in Medemblik), Dirck Graeff*(another Calvinist leader who had found it prudent to go and live in Emden), and Adriaen Pauw* (who had been living in Emden and Hamburg). For some years it was still possible for Catholics to serve on the Town Council. An example is Ysbrant Dommer,*who joined in 1578 and remained till his death in about 1582. Even when they disappeared, a group within the élite, how large a group we do not know, still stood up for religious tolera-tion. The most famous member of this group was C.P. Hooft*. With his dislike of religious persecution, on the part of Catholics or Protestants, went a dislike of subtle theological disputations and of the ambition of the clergy; his conception of Christianity as a matter of 'good conscience' rather than a matter of deep theological questions; in short, his 'interior religion' (the term *innerlycke religieusheydt* is his own). Like Sir Thomas Browne, Hooft* might have declared that 'I condemn not all things in the Council of Trent' (he owned a book by the Counter-Reformation controversialist Cardinal Baronio) 'nor approve all in the synod of Dort', the Dutch synod which declared it incumbent on Calvinists to believe that all men are totally depraved and that God has elected only a few to salvation. C.P. Hooft* married a Blaeu, and it is unlikely that the Blaeu family were strong Calvinists either. At any rate Joan Blaeu* used to print missals (with 'Cologne' on the title-page) for export to the Catholic world. Perhaps this was no more significant than the trade with Spain which Andries Bicker,* for example, engaged in, but Bicker* does not seem to have been such a strong Calvinist either, and Blaeu* once went so far as to dedicate a book to pope Alexander VII. Martin Coster* has been described as a 'fiery Calvinist', and he was certainly unorthodox enough to have to leave Amsterdam in 1566. But his library included not only Calvin (not very much at that) but works by Erasmus and Melanchthon and the decrees of the Council of Trent. Even Reynier Cant,* who was an elder of the Calvinist church, objected to attempts to drive out the Catholics after 1578, and it was said that he died a Catholic himself.[49]

In the controversy between Professor Arminius and Professor Gomarus over the deep points of grace and predestination which came to a head about the year 1608, it is tempting and not unreasonable to see an analogy with the Venetian crisis of 1606. In both cities the theology of grace had become entwined with a political question, whether the state was to control the church or not — or better, whether the patricians were to control the clergy or not. It is equally tempting, but more misleading, to take the gentle Hooft* as typical of Amsterdam

patrician attitudes, in the same way that it is both tempting and misleading to take Nicolò Contarini* as typical of Venetian ones. It is true
that Arminius himself had married into the patriciate—in 1590 he
married Lijsbeth, daughter of Laurens Reael* (father of the more
famous Admiral Dr Laurens Reael*). Other members of the élite, such
as Dirck Bas* and Albert Burgh,* supported the position of the
'Remonstrants' or followers of Arminius. It is true that the Grand
Pensionary of Holland, Oldenbarnevelt, supported both the Arminians
and the power of the Dutch regent class; that the Prince of Orange supported the Gomarists (or 'Counter-Remonstrants') and that in 1618,
when the controversy was at its height, he purged the council
of Amsterdam and other towns of supporters of Arminius. When the
Remonstrants were forced into founding a separate church, twelve
members of the Amsterdam élite (not to mention their close relatives)
had their children baptized there between 1633 and 1673. They included Hans Bontemantel,* whose political diary is such an important
source for our knowledge of the period, Henrick Hooft* (following in
the footsteps of his great-uncle C.P. Hooft*), Nicolaes van Loon,*
Willem van Loon,* and Cornelis van Vlooswijk.* [50]

All this is true, but not the whole story. The Amsterdam élite no
less than the Venetian contained a devout party of faction, *kerkelyken*
(to use the contemporary term) as well as *libertynen*. The Prince
of Orange was able to step in and purge the Town Council of
Amsterdam in 1618 partly because he had allies within it. The devout
faction was led by Reynier Pauw,* one of the key figures behind the
convocation of the synod of Dort, where the Remonstrants were ex-
communicated. Unfortunately, Pauw's* papers have not survived,
so that it is not possible to describe his religious attitudes in any
detail.[51] But we do have some evidence from his circle, for example
from Pieter Schaep.* Pieter Schaep* wrote a letter to his son when
Gerard Schaep* went up to Leyden University in 1617.[52] It is difficult
to avoid the term 'puritan' when describing the cluster of attitudes
expressed in this letter. (Oldenbarnevelt once described the Counter-
Remonstrants to the British ambassador as 'double puritans'.)
Dr Schaep* was concerned that his son should organise his studies
well, that he should avoid wasting time, drunkenness and 'whoredom',
and, above all, that he should 'Fear God'. Quotations from Proverbs
and from Ecclesiastes about the fear of the Lord echo through the letter.
Gerard Schaep's* papers have also survived. The image of God which
emerges from them is that of a Being who intervenes constantly in daily

life, a very different image from the God of C.P. Hooft,* who liked to stress man's ignorance of the divine.[53]

Thus in Calvinist Amsterdam as in Catholic Venice there was both a devout group and an anti-clerical group within the élite. Where the fear of Spain played into the hands of the Venetian anti-clericals, in Amsterdam it played into the hands of the devout. One should perhaps interpret the stern doctrines of the synod of Dort as the expression of a mood of fear, which declined, when the fear of Spain declined, in the middle of the seventeenth century. The last of the strict Calvinist in the élite was probably Nicholas Tulp,* who died in 1674 at the age of eighty-one. One might contrast two members of the Witsen family, important in the early and the late seventeenth century respectively. Gerrit Witsen* was a zealous Calvinist and a friend of Reynier Pauw. * Nicolaes Witsen* was interested in religion but in a more ecumenical way. In Russia he went to visit patriarch Nikon and he made notes on the cult of icons, the importance of St Nicholas and other details of Orthodox worship. His sympathies extended to the 'holy Confucius', and he was also interested in shamanism.[54]

It is dangerous to take Coenraad van Beuningen* as typical of anything, but he illustrates another possible religious attitude of the late seventeenth century, another rejection of strict Calvinism. He opposed Catholicism, Lutheranism and Calvinism alike as the 'three unclean spirits'; his sympathies were not with churches but with sects—the *Collegianten* of Rijnsburg, the Quakers, the Behmenists (followers of Jakob Boehme), and the followers of Labadie, another of the 'Christians without a church' of the seventeenth century.[55]

Patronage of the Arts

The differences in the style of life, attitudes and values of the patricians of Amsterdam and Venice were reflected in their patronage of the arts.

Despite their ideal of personal frugality, Venetian patricians were believers in 'magnificence', which they defined themselves in terms of 'conspicuous consumption' (a possible if free translation of *spendere largamente*). The great occasions for displaying this magnificence were 'banquets, weddings and buildings, where it is right to spend without thinking of the expense'. The point about buildings is an important one. They too were part of the 'front' of the Venetian nobleman. The architect Scamozzi described the Venetian palace as an expression of 'the style of life of the nobility' (*l'uso del vivere della nobiltà*), pointing out, for example, the importance of the main entrance, 'to be able to give receptions for the relatives when there are weddings, and to give parties and feasts'.[1] The dominant motive for all this magnificence was family pride, a sense of the 'honour' or 'splendour' of the 'house', its *honorevolezza, decoro, lustro, splendore.* The family palace was at the centre of the attention of patricians. They would dream for generations of enlarging it or redecorating it, buying up the neighbouring houses and exhorting their descendants to carry on the good work. Marin Grimani,* in his will, describes the 2,844 ducats he has spent on the *soler* or upper apartment of the palace at S. Luca, built by the famous Renaissance architect Sammicheli for his father, and he instructs his heirs to have a staircase of Veronese stone made for the main entrance. The palace was more than a place to live, it was a symbol of the family. It was surely no accident that the same term, *casa*, was used of both. Hence Antonio Grimani* wrote of his palace in his will: 'I do not want it ever to be rented out; it must be inhabited by my sons and their dependants for ever.' Zuan da Lezze* gave his heirs similar instructions not to divide, sell or rent out the palace. Some spectacular new palaces were built in seventeenth-century Venice, including Palazzo Pisani on Campo S. Stefano, built when Alvise Pisani* was head of the branch, and Palazzo Pesaro on the Grand Canal, planned by Zuan Pesaro* and built by Longhena for his nephew Lunardo Pesaro.* The branch had bought houses nearby in 1558, 1569 and

1628 in order to make possible a building on this scale. Similarly, Zuan da Lezze* declared in his will that he had spent over 34,000 ducats on the family palace (near the church of the Crutched Friars) and bought the house next door with a view to future enlargements.[2]

Sumptuous monuments, built by teams of architects and sculptors, were another way of glorifying the family. Seventeenth-century monuments quite dwarf the tombs of earlier times. The monument to Marin Grimani* at S. Iseppo cost 5,865 ducats, but this was nothing compared to the monument to Silvestro Valier* at S. Zanipolo, which cost 20,000 ducats. Portrait busts now in museums often derive from these tombs; the famous Vittoria bust of Nicolo da Ponte* is an example. A patrician might decide to give his parish church a new façade and commission sculptors to turn it into an enormous family monument. Andrea Contarini, son of Carlo Contarini,* left 10,000 ducats to rebuild the façade of S. Vidal and decorate it with the busts of his parents. Vincenzo Fini* and his brother made the façade of S. Moisè into a monument to themselves at a cost of 90,000 ducats. Even the villa in the country was turning into a palace at this time. Think of villa Corner at Poisuolo designed by Scamozzi for Zuan I Corner;* of Villa Contarini at Piazzola, enlarged by Marco Contarini;* and of the two spectacular examples from the early eighteenth-century, villa Manin at Passeriano (for the family of Ottavio Manin*) and villa Pisani at Strà, for the Pisani of S. Stefano, who contributed six members to the élite in the period. An exception to this trend was the modest villa at Conselve near Padua built by Zuan Sagredo,* but his meanness, as we have seen, was if not proverbial, at least anecdotal. Or should one say that he kept up the ancient virtue of frugality in an increasingly corrupt age?[3]

The patronage of painters and writers was rather less a matter of the honour of the house and rather more a question of personal taste, likely to reflect a genuine interest in the arts. Marcantonio Barbaro* not only employed Veronese to decorate his villa but tried his hand at sculpture. Zuan Pesaro's* love of paintings even led him to loot some on one occasion when he was in command of Venetian forces. A visitor to the house of a Venetian patrician would have been struck by the number of paintings, portraits most of all. Tintoretto painted Marcantonio Barbaro,* Pasquale Cicogna,* Polo Paruta,* Vincenzo Morosini,* and other members of the élite. Some portraits were commissioned to glorify the family. Nicolò Corner* had three portraits of his ancestress Caterina, Queen of Cyprus, and the inventory of Francesco da Molin's* paintings begins with six pictures of senators and generals of the da Molin family. Other portraits were there to gratify an interest in history: portraits of doges, of cardinals, the occasional pope, king, or even 'the Grand Turk'. Religious paintings were much in evidence. They constituted about a third of Ferigo Contarini's* collection (57 out of 153) as of Francesco da Molin's* (39 out of 136). Paintings of Christ, the Virgin, and the saints; St John the Baptist, St Francis, the Magdalen and St Sebastian were among the most popular saints, and such local favourites as St Mark, St Marina and the blessed Lorenzo Giustinian (himself a Venetian noble) also made an appearance. The rest of the collection would probably have been made up of classical mythologies, such as paintings of Venus and Apollo; of what contemporaries called 'moral inventions', allegorical paintings with titles like *Truth*, or *Time, Prudence and Fame*; and historical paintings, usually classical, like *Alexander and the Family of Darius* or *Scipio and the Spanish Slave*, both illustrating the virtues of a conqueror: clemency and continence. These were the private equivalents of the paintings of historical scenes in the Doge's Palace, which were also seen as 'examples of virtue' (*esempi virtuosi*). Giacomo Correr* had a particularly fine collection of historical paintings. There might be a few landscapes in seventeenth-century Venetian collections, but they were very much in the background of attention.[4]

Lying on his death-bed, Zuanfrancesco Loredan is said to have told his son, 'Among other obligations entailed on you I leave the patronage of *virtuosi* . . . the Venetian noble has always been the protector of literary men. 'Books were dedicated to members of the élite, to a few of them (such as Nicolò Sagredo*) in particular, and presumably the authors were rewarded. In the late seventeenth century there was a kind of unofficial poet laureate in Venice, the priest Cristoforo Ivanovitch, who used to write regular and (for modern tastes, at least) somewhat nauseating complimentary verses on the proctors and others to celebrate their marriages and political appointments. Thus he wrote a sonnet for the appointment of Girolamo Zustinian* when he became a proctor in 1675, with an appropriate reference to the eagle on the clan coat of arms; a sonnet for Girolamo Grimani* when he was made *Provveditore Generale* of Dalmatia in 1675; and many other pieces of 'poetic applause', as Ivanovitch called his products.[5]

Some of the devout faction, including Agostino Barbarigo* and Zaccaria Contarini,* in the late sixteenth century, wanted the theatres closed and the actors expelled from Venice.[6] But other patricians took a lively interest in the theatre and in music. In the later sixteenth century the aristocratic amateur theatricals of the 'shoe societies' (*compagnie delli calzi*) still existed, and Andrea Dolfin* was a member of one of these clubs in his youth. Marin Grimani* was an enthusiast for music, and Venice was one of the first cities in Europe to welcome the new art-form of the opera. The commercial opera house (that is, one to which entry was by ticket and not by invitation) was introduced to Venice in 1637. By the late seventeenth century there were twelve opera houses in Venice, of which eight were owned by noble families, including Alvise Duodo,* who opened one at S. Aponal in 1651, and Marcantonio Zustinian, in whose family theatre at S. Moisè Monteverdi's *Arianna* had its première in 1640. Marco Contarini* had a theatre and a music-room constructed on his country estate at Piazzola on the Brenta, and his collection of opera scores was a famous one. One hundred and twenty manuscript scores now in the Marciana Library in Venice come from his collection, including the scores of twenty-seven operas with music by Cavalli. Subjects from Roman history were extremely popular, Scipio and Alexander among them; in 1595 the musical drama *The triumph of Scipio* was played before the doge, Marin Grimani;* in 1651 an opera called *Alexander conqueror of himself* was performed, and in 1664 Cavalli's *Scipio Africanus*. The analogy with the paintings collected by patricians is obvious enough.[7]

The works of architecture and sculpture commissioned by the Amsterdam élite show, as one might have expected, less magnificence, less display and less desire for the conspicuous glorification of the family. There were some quite grand town houses, it is true, like the present Herengracht 446, the house of Andries de Graeff;* the house of Alexander Velters* on the Herengracht, valued at 40,000 florins; the Trippenhuis, a town hall in miniature; or the house Vingboons built on the Singel for Joan Huydecoper,* which took up the space of three houses and had a magnificent garden, with fountain and statues, which gave it the appearance, from the rear, of a country house rather than a town one. In general, the houses of the Amsterdam élite were not on the scale of the Venetian palaces, nor were they so expensive. Two houses on the Keizersgracht owned by members of the élite, Jan de Bisschop* early in the seventeenth century and Daniel Bernard* at its end, were valued at 14,000 florins each; that would be about 7,000 ducats, little enough by Venetian standards. (I omit Bernard's* stabling facilities in the nearby Blomstraat, valued at another 2,500 florins.) Other lived still more simply, like Dirk Munter* and his wife, a childless couple, in a sixth of a house on the Herengracht, valued at 3,400 florins. In Amsterdam a house was simply a place for the nuclear family to live in and does not seem to have had the symbolic importance of the Venetian palace.[8]

Nor did the Amsterdammers spend much on family tombs. It was not that the grand tomb was unknown in the Dutch Republic: the monuments to William the Silent and to Piet Hein are splendid instances to the contrary. But the sumptuous monument was not part of the style of life of the Amsterdam élite, apart from occasional exceptions. The de Graeff family had their own chapel, the former St Cornelius chapel, in the Old Church, and Cornelis de Graeff* commissioned a tomb there with sculptures by Quellin.[9]

The country houses of the Amsterdam élite seem to have been modest affairs compared with those of seventeenth century Venetians, in spite of the occasional flattering poetic reference to a 'palace'. They tended to lack columns or pilasters; most of them have disappeared, but a modest style and scale is suggested by contemporary drawings and also by the occasional valuation. Take Vredenhof, for example, the country house near Voorschoten which once belonged to Andries de Graeff.* In 1733 it was valued at 9,000 florins, including the gardens and other land round it. The inventory of 1733 lists the rooms. There was a 'great chamber' (*groote zaal*), but there were only eleven rooms altogether, including four service rooms—kitchen, cellar, servants' room and coach-house.[10]

In Amsterdam the important commissions for architects were not private but public. The great expansion of the city ensured that builders were not left unemployed. As burgomasters rather than private individuals, the de Graeffs, Bickers and others handed out commissions for the South Church (1603), the West Church (1620), the Bourse and, best known of all, the new Town Hall. Like medieval Florence or medieval Venice, patronage in seventeenth-century Amsterdam was predominantly civic.

By the later seventeenth century, if not before, Amsterdam patricians seem to have equalled Venetians in their interest in collecting pictures. Jan Six,* the patron of Rembrandt, is the most famous example, but there are many more. There was a similar interest in portraits. Gerard Schaep,* an enthusiast for family history, records an expense of 450 florins for having family portraits copied and framed.[11] More characteristic of Amsterdam, as of the Dutch Republic in general, was the group portrait — the anatomy lesson, for example, like the one Rembrandt painted for Nicolaes Tulp,* and the ones Aert Pieterszoon and Thomas de Keyser painted for another doctor in the élite, Sebastiaen Egbertszoon.* More important still as a genre was the *schutterstuk*, the painting of the civic guard in their uniforms. In the Rijksmuseum today there are ten such paintings in which the captain of the guard is one of the élite, from Jan de Bisschop* (1599) to Joan Huydecoper* (1648). These paintings were sometimes put on display in the *doelen*, or militia headquarters, but they might hang in the captain's house. Historical paintings could be found in the houses of patricians. Lucretia and Portia, for example, presumably as symbols of womanly virtue, and the Horatii, symbols of civic patriotism. There were 'moral inventions', which included the elaborate programme executed by Nicolaes Held-Stokade for Louys Trip,* including Prudence, Wisdom, Fortune and Riches, clearly a pictorial panegyric to Trip's* success in business.[12] As might have been expected, Old Testament subjects were rather more popular in Amsterdam collections than in Venetian ones: Abraham, for example, David, Joseph, and Solomon. Nor is it surprising to find much more emphasis on landscape, on still-life and on genre paintings. It is more surprising to find the occasional St Sebastian or St Stephen turning up, or to find some burgomasters collecting mythological paintings; Andries de Graeff* had paintings of Ceres, Flora, Juno, Venus and 'a naked Diana lying down' in his house. The strongly Calvinist burgomaster Tulp* once protested against the floats of 'heathen gods and goddesses' laid on to entertain the Prince of Orange; one wonders what he made of his colleague's paintings. But Tulp* was also a patron of the arts. Rembrandt's famous *Anatomy Lesson* was painted for him, and he was particularly fond of the work of Paul Potter, who specialised in painting animals in landscapes. Tulp* invited Potter to Amsterdam and owned most of his work. This contrast in collections between de Graeff* and Tulp* may furnish a little support for the argument that Calvinism indirectly encouraged the rise of landscape painting.[13]

Much the same small group of patricians also acted as patrons of literature. In the early seventeenth century the 'chambers of rhetoric', a kind of literary club, were still important in the culture of the United Provinces. The Amsterdam chamber, 'The Eglantine', included members of such patrician families as Pauw, Reael and Schaep. The brothers de Graeff;* the Huydecopers,* father and son; Jan Six;* these names recur in the dedications of the works of Vondel and of Jan Vos, a minor poet who played the same laureate's role at Amsterdam that Ivanovitch did in Venice. Amsterdam patricians, like Venetian ones, received 'poetic applause' when they married, went on embassy or were appointed burgomasters. Poems were written on their portraits or their country houses. A vast quantity of this occasional verse was produced. At least twenty-four people celebrated in Latin verse the burgomasterships and the death of Willem Backer.* As for more serious works, it is interesting to find the same mixture of biblical and classical themes in the plays written for the Amsterdam theatre as in the galleries of the Huydecopers* and the de Graeffs;* plays about David, Solomon, Medea and Claudius Civilis, the Batavian hero of resistance to Rome.[14]

It is natural to wonder whether the patricians had any influence on the plays which were dedicated to them, and what they wanted. In one case at least there is good evidence for an answer, the case of Vondel's *Palamedes.* One day in 1625 Vondel was talking to Albert Burgh* about Oldenbarnevelt, who had been executed six years before, and Burgh* said, 'Write a tragedy about it.' Vondel answered, 'It isn't the time yet.' Burgh* replied, 'Just change the name.'[15] The result was *Palamedes.* In an age accustomed to historical parallels there was no difficulty in recognizing the 'injured innocent' Palamedes as Oldenbarnevelt, Agamemnon as Maurice Prince of Orange, or Megeer as Reynier Pauw.* Vondel was called before the magistrates of Amsterdam to answer for his play. Some of them wanted him acquitted, while others, the devout faction, wanted him punished severely. In the end he was simply fined. This was not the only occasion that Vondel ran into trouble for his plays. In 1638 the church council (*kerkeraad*) complained that his play *Gysbrecht van Amstel* was 'superstitious'. Set in the Middle Ages, it contained references to Catholic beliefs. However, burgomaster Jacob de Graeff* declared that there was nothing offensive in it and the performance went ahead. Again, in 1654, the church council complained about Vondel's *Lucifer.* This time the burgomasters (one of whom was Tulp*) banned the play. The divergences between the de Graeff family and Tulp* extended to their attitudes to the drama. The Town Council was not only divided about Vondel, it was divided on the question of whether to have a theatre at all. The devout faction (like the English puritans in this respect too) wanted the theatre closed and the building turned into a school. The burgomasters tended to take a moderate line, supporting the existence of the theatre but warning the players against causing scandal. This moderation seems to have been the resultant of opposing forces. For example, in 1666, a year when the burgomasters allowed the theatre to reopen but gave the actors a stern warning, the burgomasters included Tulp* but also Vondel's patrons Cornelis van Vlooswijk* and Andries de Graeff.*[16]

Much has been written about the possible relationship between the Counter-Reformation and the baroque style, and something about Calvinism and Classicism.[17] A comparative study of the taste of two seventeenth-century patriciates, one Catholic and one predominantly Calvinist, seems an obvious way of attacking the problem.

In Venice there were influential patricians of sober tastes in the late sixteenth century, Ferigo Contarini* for example, but the taste for the ornate soon became dominant. Tintoretto had been a controversial painter, but in the next generation his follower Sante Peranda became quite fashionable for religious paintings. His patrons included such prominent members of the devout faction as Marin Grimani,* who took him to Rome in 1592, and Renier Zen,* who owned an *Agony in the Garden* and a *Scourging at the Pillar* by Peranda; Zen's* flamboyant piety is attested in other ways too. Peranda's style was admired at the time for its grace and elegance, his *maniera cosi graziosa, gentile e leggiadra.*[18] For portraits, the man was Tiberio Tinelli, a painter much influenced by van Dyck. Antonio Nani* and Antonio Priuli* owned works by Tinelli. Another fashionable painter of the time was Pietro Liberi, a pupil of Padovanino. Francesco Molin* admired Liberi's work and had the painter knighted in 1652; the Fini* family commissioned him to decorate their palace; Alvise Pisani* and Giacomo Correr* each owned a painting by him. Correr* also owned something by the 'capricious' Joseph Heinz, and a 'strangely beautiful painting' (*pittura pelegrina*) by Luca Ferrari.[19] From about 1640 onwards, the rising taste for the exuberant can be illustrated by opera, which in this period was spectacle, drama and music—in that order. The most famous of baroque sculptures, Bernini's St Teresa, was commissioned by Cardinal Ferigo Corner, son of Doge Zuan I Corner.* Tirali's monument to Silvestro Valier* (1705-8) has the whole baroque apparatus of draperies, swags and coloured marble. It was Vincenzo Fini* who commissioned the façade of S. Moisè from the architect Tremignon and the sculptor

Meyring, a Flemish follower of Bernini. Richness of decoration could hardly go further. The columns on the façade of S. Moisè are not only fluted, they have ornamental bands across them, and these bands are themselves ornamented with rosettes. It may be significant that the patrons of this truly monumental piece of expensive bad taste had been ennobled only twenty years before.

More eclectic in his tastes was Doge Nicolò Sagredo.* His will refers to some of his paintings, including two 'in the room in which I sleep', a Pietro di Cortona and a Poussin. The taste for Poussin seems an unusual one in a Venetian patrician of the period; perhaps it resulted from Sagredo's* residence in Rome as ambassador in the 1650s.

In literature, the Venetian élite were split between the taste for the ornate and difficult and the taste for the plain and simple. Pietro Basadonna* was said to be 'a lover of conceits and of pungent witticisms' (*amico delle arguzie e de'concettini frizzanti*). Zuanfrancesco Loredan was a great admirer of the baroque poet Marino, whose biography he wrote, and he cultivated what contemporaries would have called a 'conceited' style himself. A taste for the exotic is to be found in the subjects for operas and romances, and in their treatment.[21] An inflation (not to say debasement) of language was taking place; the word 'heroic' is an obvious example of this process, especially when it rolls off the pen of Cristoforo Ivanovitch, describing (for instance) the erection of a theatre at Piazzola as the result of the 'heroic genius' and the 'heroic generosity' of Marco Contarini*. Playing on words was popular, and word-play turns up in the most serious contexts. When Domenico Contarini* refers in his will to his brother's 'angelic virtues', it may come as a surprise to the modern reader to discover that his brother's name was Angelo.

Other Venetians, like Paolo Sarpi and his circle, including Nicolò Contarini* and Lunardo Donà,* wrote in a simple style. They were not alone in their tastes. The Senate did not care for Basadonna's* speeches because it preferred a 'solid and vigorous style' (*le sode e vigorose sentenze*) to a sharp and conceited one. It was the Senate too which voted for Longhena's plan for the church of the *Salute* over its rival; a plan described to them by the building committee not in terms of mass or ornament but in terms of spaciousness and light.[21] It is tempting to see the taste for the simple as corresponding to the traditional Venetian style of frugality and the taste for the ornate as associated with the new style of more conspicuous consumption. In the seventeenth century the ornate style was winning.

In Amsterdam, the plain style seems to have been dominant throughout the period, in the architecture of Vingboons and Van Campen, the landscapes of Potter, the flower pieces of the Van Huysums, or the portraits of Van de Helst. Van de Helst seems to have been the most fashionable portrait painter for the Amsterdam élite between the 1640s and the 1660s; his sitters included Daniel Bernard,* Frans Banningh Cocq* (who is best known for his appearance in Rembrandt's more flamboyant *Night Watch*), Joan Huydecoper,* Albert Pater,* Cornelis de Vlooswijk* and Cornelis Witsen.* His works are perceptive but they do not seem to idealize their subjects. The artist and writer Houbraken specifically mentions the lack of ornament on the houses designed by Philips Vingboons, for example the house he built at Pijnenburgh near Utrecht for the widow of Jacob Hinlopen.* [22]

A small group of patricians seems to have been attracted by a grander style. Andries de Graeff* (besides sitting to Rembrandt and quarrelling over the price) employed the painter Jacob Jordaens and the sculptor Artus Quellin, both baroque in style and, significantly, from Antwerp; he was on friendly terms with the painter Govert Flinck, who borrowed elegant poses from Van Dyck to make his sitters look more aristocratic. For example, Flinck painted a portrait of an unidentified member of the Munter family (which contributed four members to the élite) in which the sitter has one hand to his breast and the other elegantly drooping.[23]

Coenraed van Beuningen,* eccentric as usual, fits neither category; his tastes in painting were for Dürer and for Bles. But the general impression left by Amsterdam patrician taste is predominantly sober with a dash of something grander, an impression summed up by the Town Hall, a plain building whose simple lines do not harmonize with the enormous pediments full of allegorical sculpture, again the work of Artus Quellin. The taste for the difficult in literature seems to have been more widespread than the taste for the ornate in painting. Puns, anagrams and acrostics were all popular in the literature addressed to the élite. For Peter Schaep* (Petrus Schaepius) someone composed the anagram *'tu spe hic superas'*. When Vos wrote an epitaph on Abraham Boom* he could not resist the obvious reference to a tree (*boom*), and his epitaph on Albert Burgh* calls him the 'people's stronghold' (*Burgerburg*). Nor can he describe Marsseveen, the villa of his chief patron, Joan Huydecoper,* without a flattering pun on 'Mars and Venus'.[24]

Training

This chapter is concerned with education, not in the relatively narrow sense of the formal training offered by schools and universities, though this of course is included, but in the wider sense of 'socialization', the whole process by which an older generation passes on its culture to a younger, starting from birth.

All too little is known about the early years of noble Venetians, and the remarks which follow are necessarily impressionistic and even speculative. However, the subject is too important to leave out. We have seen that the aristocratic household in Venice was often a large one, including not only brothers and sisters but also uncles and many servants. The father might be absent because he was serving as a naval officer, an ambassador, or a *rettore* on the mainland. This is the situation, for example, underlying a letter written in 1540 by a noble Venetian lady to her husband, absent in Cyprus, giving him news of their five children: 'Lunardo is learning very well and I believe that we can expect well of him . . . . Antonio . . . is beginning to speak and is my solace.' 'Lunardo', then aged four, is the famous Doge Lunardo Donà* who has often occurred in these pages.[1] Mention has already been made of Zuan Dolfin, who left the church to look after his younger brother when his father was employed away from Venice. The Venetian noble child would be brought up by his father, when he was there; his mother; and also by his uncles, the older siblings, and the servants. There are reasons for surmising that he would be given to a wet-nurse (not suckled by his mother) and that he would be weaned late (by modern standards), at about the age of two.[2]

The Venetian noble child would be aware of hierarchy right from the start because of the strict hierarchy within the household in which he was growing up. Servants, women and younger brothers all knew their places. The child would not make great emotional investments in any one member of the household but rather in the whole group. His training was more likely to be strict early in the period than at its end. The traditional training, as described by the nobleman Francesco Barbaro in the middle of the fifteenth century, was to bring children up to eat and drink relatively little, to keep silent and to restrain themselves from 'excessive laughter'. This style of training certainly fits in with the behaviour of well-known adult patricians at the beginning of the seventeenth century. However changes seem to have taken place in the course of the century; one late-seventeenth century observer, a Frenchman, noted the 'liberty' with which the children of nobles were then brought up. Another Frenchman commented that fathers, mothers and servants all idolised noble children, who therefore grew up proud, violent and accustomed to having their own way. In short, they were given a warm secure upbringing which would tend to discourage them from leaving the family palace. An extended family is likely to discourage the desire for achievement, since the individual is never thrown on his own resources. The mechanism is likely to be the more effective when the family is a noble one, for a nobleman's sense of identity depended on his 'house', not on his own achievements.[3]

As for formal education, it was remarked by a foreign visitor that in Venice 'the higher nobility . . . usually have their children educated at home by private tutors.' Silvestro Valier* and Zuan II Corner* certainly fitted this pattern. Education outside the home was dominated by the religious orders, with the significant exception of the most famous teaching order of the period, the Jesuits. Noble girls might be sent to convents. Noble boys might be taught by the Dominicans, as Battista Nani* was, or by the Somaschi, as Francesco Molin* was. They might be sent outside Venice. Francesco Morosini* was sent to the seminary of S. Carlo at Modena, a training which seems not to have hindered him from making the most successful naval career of the century.[4]

At the age of about sixteen the young man might go on to university. One girl did too, the famous bluestocking Elena Lucrezia Corner, the illegitimate daughter of Zuanbattista Corner.* University, for a Venetian, meant Padua; they were forbidden to study elsewhere, though this prohibition did not prevent Lunardo Donà* from studying briefly at Bologna in 1555. How many of the élite went to Padua it is unfortunately impossible to say, but at least eight out of the twenty-five doges of the period did so. This proportion, about 30 per cent, may be typical of the upper nobility from whom the doges and proctors were usually drawn. Many of the lower nobility were ill-educated; indeed, if contemporary comment can be trusted, they were near-illiterate. Studying at Padua was expensive. Nicolò Contarini,* whose branch of that famous clan were not well off, may be described as having work-

ed his way through Padua; he was a *camerlengo*, a minor Venetian
official, in Padua when he was twenty.[5]

The most popular subjects of study at Padua were rhetoric, philosophy and law. Philosophy meant scholastic philosophy; the local Paduan
brand of Aristotelianism was still strong in the seventeenth century.
Between 1591 and 1631 the celebrated Cesare Cremonini taught there.
His salary was double that of Galileo, and the Venetian Senate described him as 'the honour of Padua university', although he was three times
investigated by the inquisition for alleged unorthodoxy; for a secret
seminar on the mortality of the soul, for a joke at the expense of
the devout who went to kiss the tomb of St Anthony at Padua, and for
his view that God was remote from the working of the universe. He
was in a position where he could influence young men who would later
be prominent in Venetian life, and the attitudes of Zuanfrancesco
Loredan and his circle may owe something to Cremonini's example.[6]

This was the formal education of a patrician, but informal education was important too. Whether they could read or write, Venetian
nobles learned what a contemporary unkindly described as 'a certain
style and a soft way of speaking accompanied by a grave manner which
takes people in with ease'.[7] No more than in Oxford or Cambridge in
the seventeenth century did the young gentlemen at Padua give their
attention exclusively to the academic curriculum. There were riding-
schools, fencing-schools and dancing-schools at Padua from the very
beginning of the period. Some Venetian fathers were well aware of the
value of travel as a form of education, as a form of political education
in particular. Domenico Contarini* and his brother Anzolo Contarini,*
one a doge and the other a well-known diplomat, were sent abroad when
young to gain experience of the courts of princes, 'so that we would be
fit and able to govern the commonwealth well'. Similarly, Francesco
Contarini* travelled in France, Spain and Portugal, and Ferigo Corner*
travelled in France, Spain and Germany. It was not uncommon for
young men of good families to travel in the suite of an ambassador.
Giacomo Foscarini* visited France in this way, and Pietro Basadonna*
visited Istanbul.[8]

Another form of 'political novitiate', as one contemporary called it,
was institutionalised; it was appointment as *savio agl'ordini* at about
the age of twenty-five to learn about affairs by listening to the discussions of the College. Thus Lunardo Donà,* Agostino Nani* and
Bertucci Valier* were appointed *savi* at the age of twenty-five; Marcantonio Barbaro* at the unusually early age of twenty-three; and

Nicolò da Ponte at about twenty-two. This political novitiate was an obvious means for the well-connected young man to get ahead of his contemporaries in the race for office. Access to special training is a well-known means by which an aristocracy remains in power over the generations. There were five of these *savi* at a time, and they held office for six months each. It was possible to serve again, and Francesco Erizzo* had three spells in the office.[9] A last type of informal education, which might start as early as twelve years old, was service at sea as *nobile di galera*, a kind of midshipman learning how to command. Two posts were reserved for young nobles on each galley, and six on each galeass. The naval careers of Zuan Bembo* and Francesco Morosini,* among others, started in this way.[10]

In Amsterdam as in Venice we know next to nothing about the all-important early years of training, but the scraps of information available suggest a considerable contrast between the two cities. In Amsterdam the child of a member of the élite would be brought up in a relatively small household without uncles and without many servants. The household would be a more democratic society than was the case in Venice. The position of Dutch wives and servants was a relatively favourable one which tended to surprise foreign visitors.[11] It is reasonable to suspect less use of the wet-nurse in Amsterdam than in Venice, because servants were fewer; and earlier weaning, because there was less use of the wet-nurse. It has been suggested that early weaning leads to anxiety in the infant, anxiety to greed, greed to ambition in the adult, and ambition to achievement.[12] Whether this is so or not, the Amsterdam élite were achievers, and greed was more characteristically their vice than the vice of the Venetians. One should add that in their smaller households each individual would feel more need to achieve than the Venetians simply to survive economically; and that since they were commoners, their identity depended more on their achievements than the identity of noble Venetians. Education was probably stricter in Amsterdam than in Venice. Calvinists tended to see little children as wicked, an idea associated with their stress on original sin, and so they were likely to be strict in bringing up children in the 'fear of the Lord'.[13] Body shame was more developed in Dutch society than elsewhere in Europe. Nicolaes Witsen,* on a visit to Russia, recorded his shock at seeing men and women bathing naked, 'like animals, without shame'. The extraordinary cleanliness of Dutch houses made a great impression on visitors from England and France; it is therefore likely that the virtues of cleanliness and order were instilled into the children at an early age, and helped form orderly adults.[14] In short, it is tempting to compare the childhood of the Amsterdammers with that of the Yurok Indians as brilliantly described by Erik Erikson; however different the two social structures, we find the same stress on thrift and cleanliness. The Yurok were a society of salmon fishers, and the wealth of Amsterdam too was founded on fish—on the trade in herring.[15]

1578 is a significant date in the history of Amsterdam education for negative reasons: the monastic schools were abolished, leaving only private schools and the 'public gymnasia' or grammar schools on the 'Old Side' and the 'New Side' of Amsterdam. The one on the Old Side was the more famous; in the early seventeenth century the best-known of the teachers was a Devonshire man, Matthew Slade, at one time a Brownist. The Town Council took a considerable interest in the school, appointing 'scholarchs' from its own members to govern it; Gerard Schaep,* for example, Nicolaes Tulp,* Jacob de Graeff,* Cornelis de Graeff.* Some of the élite certainly studied there: Willem Backer,* for example, Nicolaes Tulp,* Nicolaes Witsen* and Coenraed van Beuningen.* Lists of pupils survive from 1685 onwards, which show that the school then contained about two hundred pupils and that there were a good many patrician names among them. Competition was encouraged by the award of prizes. Thus in 1704 Joannes Corver, from the famous family of burgomasters, received the prize for diligence, with a special report on his ability and his spurring on the other pupils.[16] Some idea of the proficiency in Latin and of the values instilled at the school emerges from the verses recited publicly by a star pupil at the beginning of the academic year, and then published, for example, the encomium on the VOC delivered by Jan Backer* then aged sixteen in 1678, or the 'metrical oration' on the need for civic harmony delivered by Jan Trip* in 1681. It was also possible to learn 'a little Greek' there, as Nicolaes Witsen* records in his autobiography. All this evidence refers to the later part of the period. The earlier period is much more obscure; though we know from his papers that C.P. Hooft* (born in 1547) was able to quote Livy freely in Latin, we do not know whether he was typical or exceptional.

From school, over a third of the élite went on to university, the most obvious choice being Leyden, which had been founded in 1575; over 50 of the group studied there. But there was no compulsion to go to

Leyden, and Amsterdam fathers might send their sons to Franeker University in Friesland (at least eight did so) or to a university abroad; Martin Coster* studied at Ferrara, Pieter Schaep* at Heidelberg, Gerard Schaep* at Orléans, Volckert Overlander* at Basel, Andries de Graeff* at Poitiers, Francois de Vicq* at Padua. The most popular subject of study was law. At Leyden, 30 of the élite matriculated in law, 10 in philosophy, 8 in 'letters', and Frans Reael* in 1637 matriculated in history, an unusual choice at the time, though history lectures were given at Leyden in the period by scholars of high calibre such as Lipsius, Merula and Heinsius. That interest in history which we have seen was a characteristic of the group was certainly encouraged by their university training.[18]

From 1632 onwards there was an institution of higher education at Amsterdam itself: the Athenaeum. It seems to have been used as a stage between school and university; in the late seventeenth century the top class at the Latin school might pass straight on to the Athenaeum. The lists of students for the whole century have disappeared, but it is plausible to conjecture that more of the élite studied there, at home, than went on to Leyden. What made the Athenaeum especially important was its curriculum. A new institution can more easily teach new subjects and drop old ones than a traditional institution. The Athenaeum was inaugurated with Barlaeus teaching philosophy and Vossius teaching history. Both were Arminians (Barlaeus had lost his teaching post at Leyden for this reason), which shows which faction was in the ascendancy at Amsterdam in 1632. The inaugural lectures of both professors suggest a pragmatic approach to their respective subjects; Barlaeus spoke on 'the wise merchant' (*mercator sapiens*), and Vossius on 'the use of history'. The natural sciences soon became an important part of the curriculum at the Athenaeum. In the middle of the seventeenth century mathematics, astronomy, botany and medicine were all being taught there. We know that Nicolaes Witsen* studied astronomy there. Some of the teachers were sympathetic to Descartes and his philosophy at a time when he was considered a dangerous innovator elsewhere, in Leyden as in France. Professor de Raey, who taught at the Athenaeum from 1669 on, tried to make a synthesis of Aristotle and Descartes, and later the supporters of Descartes seem to have triumphed, since an edition of the works of Descartes was published in 1694 for the use of the Athenaeum students. An interest in the natural sciences; sympathy for intellectual innovation (p. 77 above); a Cartesian cast of mind—all these things were encouraged, if not implanted, by the teachers at the Athenaeum.[19]

There was also one political institution in Amsterdam with a function not unlike the post of *savio agl'ordini* at Venice. This was the 'secretary', a junior appointment often held by young men of patrician family, sometimes years before they entered the Town Council themselves. Thus Coenraed van Beuningen* was secretary when he was twenty-one, and entered the Council when he was thirty-eight; Gerrit Hooft* was secretary when he was twenty-four, and entered the Council at thirty; Cornelis Munter* was secretary at twenty-four and councillor at forty-nine. Travel was an important kind of informal education in Amsterdam as in Venice. It might be for business reasons—C.P. Hooft* travelled 'eastwards', as he put it, probably to Koenigsberg, spending three or four years there when he was an apprentice merchant (*iong coopgesel*) in his early twenties. In other cases the travel was more politically oriented. Coenraed van Beuningen* went to Paris in 1642, aged twenty, as a secretary to the celebrated Grotius, and Nicolaes Witsen* went to Moscow in 1664, aged twenty-three, in the suite of the ambassador, Jacob Boreel.* Others made the Grand Tour (*groote tour, speelreis*), with or without a tutor. In 1591 the famous scholar Lipsius went abroad as tutor to seven young Netherlanders, including the twenty-year-old Jacob de Graeff.* Jacob's son Cornelis de Graeff* went to Paris in his twenties. Joan Huydecoper* the younger went to France and Italy. On his return from Russia, Nicolaes Witsen* visited (among other places) Paris, Milan, Florence, Rome, Geneva and Frankfurt.

It is likely that both the Venetians and the Amsterdammers were, for both economic and political reasons, more widely travelled than most governing élites in seventeenth-century Europe, in spite of the growing fashion for the Grand Tour. Early travel might be regarded as socialization into tolerance, which would help to explain the remarkable stress on that value among both patriciates.

From Entrepreneur to Rentier

In every chapter so far there have been references to changes over time. These changes deserve a chapter to themselves, describing the differences between the patricians of Amsterdam and Venice in 1580 and the patricians of those two cities in 1720. The obvious question to ask, one which has been asked ever since the seventeenth century itself, is whether Venice and Amsterdam 'declined'. 'Decline' is a concept which historians would find it difficult to do without, but it is, none the less, a rather vague term. It is necessary to make all sorts of distinctions before one can use it with confidence. Did the cities of Venice and Amsterdam decline or did their élites decline? Was the decline a fall in numbers, a fall in wealth, or a fall in power? Was the decline absolute or relative?

Let us look at numbers first. In Venice, where the élite was the upper part of a formally-defined nobility, demographic decline was visible enough. The Venetian noblemen over twenty-five (that is, of an age to join the Greater Council) numbered 1,967 in 1594, but their numbers had gone down to 1,703 by the year 1719. A hundred new families had joined the nobility in the meantime, adding 316 individuals over twenty-five in 1719, so the decline in the older families was a steep one, from 1,967 to 1,387. It should be added that the new families lacked the clan organization of the old ones; the new families in 1719 averaged 3 adult males per surname, the old families averaged 12.[1]

One reason for this decline in numbers was plague, in particular the plague of 1630-31, since the choice of 1580 as a base-line means that the effects of the other great plague, that of 1575-7, have already been taken into account. Venice as a whole recovered from the plague in the sense that its population went up again to its former level, about 140,000; the nobility did not. It may be that Venice recovered its former size only as a result of immigration, and that families of native-born Venetians were generally reduced in numbers; there has been no study of this problem. But in the case of the nobility, historians have been attracted by one explanation given at the time, that the numbers of nobles were falling because fewer of them were marrying.

A case-study of 21 Venetian noble families showed that in the sixteenth century, 51 per cent of noblemen reaching marriageable age did not marry; in the seventeenth century, the proportion rose to 60 per cent, and in the eighteenth century, it would rise to 66 per cent.[2]

Another change in the structure of the Venetian nobility was the local equivalent of the 'inflation of honours' well known for seventeenth-century England. During the wars with the Ottoman Empire over Crete, in the middle of the century, and over the Morea, towards its end, the government was in great need of money and allowed new families to join the nobility. The price was 100,000 ducats. Even a family who sold sausages and came from Bergamo (the Minelli) was acceptable to the government at that price, a fact which caused great bitterness among the nobles of old stock. It was also possible to buy proctorships, for 20,000 or 25,000 ducats. There were about twice as many proctors in 1719 as there had been in 1578, and some of them had held no other important offices. What is especially striking, in a gerontocracy like Venice, is the selling of five proctorships to teenagers, one in 1649 to the doge's son, Silvestro Valier,* and the other four in the 1690s, when lack of men to fill offices as well as lack of money was becoming an acute problem for the Venetian government. However, the old noble families virtually monopolized these honours. Only five members of new families became proctors in the period.[3]

In the Dutch Republic the patriciates of some towns, Zierikzee for example, had problems of declining numbers not unlike that of Venice, but Amsterdam was not one of them. The city continued to grow until about 1680, and the number of offices to be filled was small compared with Venice. In fact the tendency at Amsterdam in the late seventeenth century was for the élite to close; of forty new burgomasters chosen between 1696 and 1748, only three were not related to previous burgomasters. There was no decline in power for families like the Corvers.[4]

The patricians of Venice and Amsterdam do not seem to have declined in wealth during the period. In Venice in 1581, the 18 members of the élite who filled in returns of their income averaged 1,300 ducats a year, and in 1711, the 38 who filled in returns averaged 7,500 ducats a year. It is difficult to know quite what to make of these figures; it is unlikely that they represent a simple increase of nearly six-fold in the wealth of the Venetian upper nobility. One has to allow something for the fall in the value of money, at least from 1581 to about

1620; and something for the fact that the increasing sale of proctor-ships drew rich men into the élite. One may also suspect, without being able to verify the hypothesis, that the difference in incomes declared in 1581 and 1711 is very largely the difference between a group which has a good deal of capital invested in trade (capital which does not appear in the returns) and a group which derives the bulk of its income from the ownership of land and houses. Even so the élite does not seem to be in economic decline; it was not the élite but the city which declined, from a port of European importance to a port of regional importance. And even then, it was not so much that Venice changed as that Venice stayed the same while the world round it changed: the Dutch and English entered the Mediterranean, and the Mediterranean declined because of the new importance of the Atlantic.[5]

In Amsterdam the spectacular increase in the wealth of the richest citizens (including the élite) was real as well as apparent. Amsterdam was not a rich or populous city in 1585, when the population was around 30,000 and only 65 households had their property assessed at 10,000 florins or more. It was both in 1674, when the population was nearing 200,000 and 259 households were assessed at 100,000 florins or more. The wealth of the city continued to increase beyond the limits of our period (to about the year 1730) and the élite continued to have a good share in that wealth.

Where then is the decline? Was there one? What contemporaries fastened on was a change in the style of life of the two élites, which they often interpreted as a moral decline, a change (to revert to the language of Pareto) from a group of entrepreneurs to a group of rentiers. Did this change really happen? If so, when did it happen, and why?[6]

It is convenient to begin with the seventeenth-century answers to these questions. About 1612, the British ambassador, Dudley Carleton, described the Venetian nobility as follows:

> They here change their manners . . . . Their former course of life was merchandising; which is now quite left and they look to land-ward buying house and lands, furnishing themselves with coach and horses, and giving themselves the good time with more show and gallantry than was wont . . . their wont was to send their sons upon galleys into the Levant to accustom them to navigation and to trade. They now send them to travel and to learn more of the gentleman than the merchant.

In 1620 an anonymous contemporary, writing in Italian, suggested that the Venetian nobles now stay at home idly instead of travelling to the Levant and that they have turned to the exploitation of the lands of the mainland to the great loss of the subject population'.[7]

As for the Netherlands, the Dutch historian Aitzema records the complaint, made at Amsterdam in 1652, 'that the regents were not merchants, that they did not take risks on the seas but derived their income from houses, lands and securities [*renten*], and so allowed the sea to be lost'. The passage has been quoted many times in discussions of Dutch social history in the last hundred years.[8]

In other words, contemporaries remarked a very important shift in the style of life of the two élites in the course of the seventeenth century. The shift was from sea to land, from work to play, from thrift to conspicuous consumption, from entrepreneur to rentier, from bourgeois to aristocrat.

Before going on to discuss possible explanations for this shift, we had better take John Selden's excellent advice. 'The reason of a thing is not to be enquired after, till you are sure the thing itself is so. We commonly are at what's the reason of it? before we are sure of the thing.' Did the shift really take place? Contemporaries are not always right about social processes in the countries they visit or even in the countries in which they live. In the early sixteenth century, a diarist from the Venetian noble clan of the Priuli had complained in much the same terms as Carleton that the Venetian nobility was deserting the sea for the land and preferring pleasure to work. About 1600 the Venetian *capitano* of Padua declared that a third of the land in the Padovano was owned by Venetians; but the same statement had been made before, in 1446. Indeed, Venetians had already bought considerable amounts of land near Padua by the end of the thirteenth century. Come to that, Venetian nobles owned land on the North Italian mainland in the ninth century. Thus the shift from entrepreneur to rentier begins to sound something like the rise of the middle class; it is described as happening in so many periods that one begins to wonder whether it ever happened at all.[9]

As for Amsterdam, the historians who have quoted the famous passage from Aitzema have not always remembered that it does not represent the considered verdict of this sober-minded and meticulous chronicler.[10] He records it as a complaint made by some Amsterdam merchants in the first year of the first Anglo-Dutch war to the effect that the war was not being prosecuted firmly enough and that their interests were being neglected. They were making a political case, not trying to describe social change. In fact, if one looks at the occupations of the members of the Town Council in 1652, it is to find that 18 out of the 37 were merchants or manufacturers, and another 8 were directors of the VOC or the West India Company, leaving only 11 men who were neither, of whom the best-known was burgomaster Cornelis de Graeff.* Once again, scepticism is in order.[11]

Another approach to the problem of whether the shift from entrepreneur to rentier really occurred is to look at specific families. This is not easy to do for Venice, where information about the trading activities of nobles is so scrappy, though one might contrast Zuanbattista Donà, merchant to the Levant, with his son Lunardo Donà,* whose wealth was derived in the main from lands in the neighbourhood of Verona.[12] The study of changes within individual families has been taken much further in the case of Amsterdam. For example, historians like to point to three generations of the de Graeff family. Dirck Graeff* was an iron-merchant, who became a burgomaster in 1578. His son Jacob was also a merchant, but he bought the manor of Zuidpolsbroek and styled himself Jacob de Graeff,* Vrijheer van Zuidpolsbroek. He was burgomaster from 1613 onwards. Two of Jacob's sons were the famous brothers Andries and Cornelis de Graeff.* They were not merchants at all but rentiers and politicians. Nicolaes Elias Pickenoy's famous portrait of Cornelis de Graeff* shows him dressed as a gentleman in a brocade doublet with lace collar and cuffs, and in hose, not in a merchant's gown. Again, one can look at three generations of the celebrated Bicker family. Gerrit Bicker,* who became burgomaster in 1603, was a brewer. His son, the famous Andries Bicker,* who became burgomaster in 1627, was a merchant in the Russia trade. He had an estate and used the title Heer van Engelenberg, but his portrait, by van de Helst, shows him plainly dressed and severe in expression. Dutch historians like to contrast this portrait with one of Andries Bicker's* son Gerard, who looks fat and dissolute and in fact came to nothing. Another well-known contrast in lives and portraits is that between C.P. Hooft,* merchant and burgomaster, in his long sober gown, and his son P.C. Hooft, historian and poet, who did not follow his father into trade or city politics but lived like a gentleman in the castle of Muiden.

All these changes in life-style over two or three generations are clear enough, and more examples could be given, but it is important not to confuse what is happening to a family with what is happening to a social group. The Graafland family, for instance, showed the same pattern of social mobility and changing style of life as the de Graeffs, but a full century later. Cornelis Graafland,* the first of his family to enter the Town Council, was an iron-merchant, just like Dirck Graeff.* He was the son of an immigrant to Amsterdam, a chest-maker who came from Rotterdam. Cornelis Graafland entered the Council in 1667. His son Joan Graafland,* born in 1652, went to university, married into the Valckenier family, one of the most famous in the patriciate of Amsterdam, and became a burgomaster in 1703. His son Gillis Graafland* became Heer van Mijnden, where he owned a country house.

The moral is that it is not enough to take individual examples; to study the problem of 'aristocratisation', or the shift from entrepreneur to rentier, it is necessary to adopt a more quantitative approach. Two facts about the élite which lend themselves to measurement are whether or not they have an occupation and whether or not they have a country house. The entrepreneur is more likely to have an occupation but no country house; the rentier, to have a country house but no occupation. The rule is not infallible; if the differences between the two groups are defined in terms of attitude, it is perfectly possible to find an entrepreneur landowner (such as Jacob Poppen*), as well as rentier without a place in the country. All the same, the chances are that an increase in the ownership of country houses and a decrease in recorded occupations between them indicate a shift from entrepreneur to rentier. The trend is as follows: [14]

Period	Without occupation	With country house
1618-50	33%	10%
1650-72	66%	41%
1672-1702	55%	30%
1702-48	73%	81%

These figures suggest that the shift did take place; that it was gradual, not sudden; and that the predominance of the rentier came not around 1650 (as the Aitzema quotation suggests) but around 1700. It seems to have been associated with an increasing interest in the arts.

It is unfortunate that a similar quantitative approach cannot be attempted in the case of Venice, but there all the patricians owned land at the beginning of the period as well as at its end; they were all noble so they did not describe their employment; although some of them engaged in trade, directly or indirectly, the tax returns offer no information about it. However, there is some evidence for a shift out of trade into land in this period.[15]

There were forces pushing the Venetian élite out of trade and forces pulling them into land. The loss of Cyprus in 1570 was a blow to trade; so was the appearance of English and Dutch ships, combining trade and piracy, in the Mediterranean and the Adriatic from about 1580 onwards; so was the appearance of the Barbary pirates and of the Uskoks, who operated from bases on the Dalmatian coast. Another blow to trade was the failure of the last private bank, owned by members of the Pisani and Tiepolo clans, in 1584. We know something of the impact of the loss of Cyprus on one member of the élite, Francesco Corner,* who owned sugar plantations on the island. He was making his will when news of the loss reached him and he had to change some of his dispositions. As for the pull into land, there is the fact that wheat prices trebled at Venice between 1550 and 1590. Venetians did eat wheat; they protested against millet loaves in 1570. The increasing power of the Ottoman Empire endangered corn imports from Eastern Europe, and so made it good business to grow corn on the mainland.[16]

For these reasons it is likely that Venetian nobles, including members of the élite, moved into land in the late sixteenth and early seventeenth centuries, while retaining the active attitudes of entrepreneurs. There was a burst of land reclamation on the Venetian mainland in this period, in which noble consortia were predominant, consortia which included such members of the élite as Ferigo Contarini* and Luca Michiel.* By 1636 Venetians owned 38 per cent of the Padovano, compared with 33 per cent in 1600.[17] However, the land boom did not last long. The economic depression of the seventeenth century, which affected most of Europe, was already noticeable in the Veneto in the 1610s, and in 1630-31 it was reinforced by plague, which quickly reduced the population under Venetian rule from about 1,700,000 to about 1 million. The rural population recovered by about 1690, but the impression remains that the great Venetian landowners took less interest in their estates as enterprises than they had been doing, that they developed rentier attitudes. It was in the late 1620s that Renier Zen* delivered a famous speech in the Greater Council against trade. Colluraffi's early seventeenth-century treatise on the education of a Venetian nobleman warns the reader against trade as a distraction from the more important business of politics. An anonymous treatise sometimes attributed to Sarpi also recommends nobles to keep out of trade, and in the late seventeenth century a treatise by the Cretan nobleman Zuanantonio Muazzo comments on the shift from trade to land and explains it by a desire for more secure, if smaller incomes.[18] The evidence from the design of villas points in the same direction. The architect Scamozzi distinguished between two kinds of villa: the smaller villa, where the farm is close to the owner's living quarters so that he can easily see what is going on, and the larger villa, where the living quarters are quite isolated from the rest. From villa Maser, which belonged to Marcantonio Barbaro* (died 1595) and in which the stables and the rooms for wine-making are part of the central ensemble, to villa Manin or villa Pisani at Strà, where there are no farm-buildings near the living quarters, the trend is clear enough. The villa-farm was re-placed by the villa-palace.[19] The rise in importance of the steward or manager, already referred to (p. 53f. above) is part of the same shift.

In short, it seems as though the change from entrepreneur attitudes to rentier attitudes was a general one in both élites. In Venice it took place about 1630, and in Amsterdam towards 1700—in each case the shift should be dated later than has usually been customary. But why did it take place at all? There are two obvious possibilities which need to be discussed in turn: explanations in terms of external and internal factors. In each case the explanation will be an example of what Fernand Braudel would call 'unconscious history', in the sense that the two élites never intended to change their attitudes or their style of life. An occasional seventeenth-century Venetian, like Michele Foscarini or Zuanantonio Muazzo, might notice the decline of noble marriages and even relate this to the decline of trade, but it is unlikely that this entered into the calculations of the individuals and families concerned. There are not many societies where men as they act can see themselves as forming part of a general social trend. At the same time, it should be stressed that the changes we are discussing were not imposed on the two groups by necessity; there were other possible reactions or possible strategies for them. A given patrician did not have to buy land or invest in the public debt; he did this because it seemed the wisest course at the time. He knew why he was taking this decision, but he was not aware of all its consequences, for his own family and the families of his contemporaries who were making similar decisions at the same time.[20]

The first possible explanation of the shift from entrepreneur to rentier is one in terms of internal factors. The essence of the process was summed up by Adam Smith when he wrote that 'merchants are commonly ambitious of becoming country gentlemen'.[21] Merchants were entrepreneurs; they were a group oriented towards achievement; they were not the group of highest status in society; they took the highest group, the nobility, as a 'reference group' or cultural model; but the nobility were rentiers. So, in pre-industrial Europe, a successful bourgeois would tend to turn into a nobleman, or his son would. It is easy to illustrate this process from the history of England, France or Spain in the sixteenth and seventeenth centuries. Merchants would buy land, acquire titles and then leave trade. From this point of view, what is surprising is not the shift but the fact that it was delayed so long in both Venice and Amsterdam. One can explain this delay by the fact that both cities were situated in republics, where there were no kings with court nobilities to imitate, and by the fact that both cities were situated away from good land, so that the two élites were almost forced into more productive investments. But these obstacles could only delay the shift, they could not halt it altogether.

This explanation seems to work quite well for Amsterdam. In the Dutch Republic the Amsterdam élite was not the group of highest status. Although there was no king there was a nobility surrounding the stadholder at his court at the Hague, which could act as a reference group for the Amsterdam merchants. The merchant might change his own style of life. A mission abroad might lead to his being knighted by a foreign monarch. The temptation to live in a style appropriate to his knighthood was a considerable one. If he did not change his own life-style, as (for example) Sir Reynier Pauw* apparently did not, he might still want his children to do better than himself socially and bring them up to do so, sending them to the Athenaeum or to university. At least three of the élite took their doctorates and then went into trade; Dr Cornelis van Dronckelaer,* Dr Jan ten Grootenhuys* and Dr Gerard van Hellemont.* These men were *mercatores sapientes* indeed, but they were exceptional. In general, higher education unfitted men to follow their fathers into the family business. The social mechanism is a well-known one. The Medici are a famous example, and it is interesting to find P.C. Hooft writing a book on the Medici and contrasting Cosimo, a rich man and an intelligent one but not well educated, with his grandson Lorenzo, patron of literature and a poet himself but not interested in business. It is difficult to resist the impression that Hooft was thinking of his father and himself.[22] The process could not be summed up more elegantly and more brutally than in an eighteenth-century Japanese *haiku*;

> House for sale
> He writes in fine Chinese style
> The third generation.[23]

In the case of Venice, this kind of explanation does not work so well. The Venetian élite were part of a formally defined nobility. They had no reference group outside themselves, unless it was the nobles of the North Italian mainland. The Venetians acquired an empire in North Italy in the fifteenth century. Gradually the Venetian nobles came to buy more land and they came to resemble the nobles of the mainland in their style of life and in their values. As China assimilated the invading Mongols and Manchus, so the mainland of North Italy assimilated the invading Venetians. Land began as servant and ended master.

In the case of Amsterdam, internal factors seem to explain the curve of development within individual families such as the de Graeffs or the Bickers or the Hoofts; they do not explain changes in the group as a whole so satisfactorily. In the case of Venice, we have already been driven to offer some kind of external explanation. However, the most obvious explanation of social change in terms of external factors involves looking at the economy. As Pareto put it, periods of economic growth are favourable to entrepreneur élites, while periods of economic stagnation or depression are favourable to rentiers. If a period of growth is followed by a period of depression, there are two possibilities: either the ruling group will modify its attitudes and behaviour, or it will be replaced by another group. The classic formulation of the dilemma is Lampedusa's *The Leopard*, where a younger-generation aristocrat, Tancredi, tells an older-generation aristocrat, Fabrizio, 'we have to change everything in order to keep everything as it is' (*se vogliamo che tutto rimanga come è, bisogna che tutto cambi*). The adaptation is not always as conscious as that, but one might argue that in economic hard times, a natural reaction is one of contempt for trade; men will not only shift their investments, but their social attitudes too. Throughout Europe the seventeenth century was an age of economic depression or crisis, so it is not surprising to find the shift from entrepreneur to rentier taking place. In the case of Venice, recently described as passing through a long commercial crisis between 1602 and 1669, this explanation does seem rather plausible. In fact there was a vicious circle. Since trade was declining, the nobles moved out of it, and since the nobles were moving out of it, trade declined. When Addison visited Venice at the beginning of the eighteenth century, he suggested that Venetian trade was falling off because 'their nobles think it below their quality to engage in traffic', while 'the merchants that are grown rich buy their nobility and generally give over trade'.[24]

In the case of Amsterdam, it is necessary to be rather more cautious. The Dutch economy in general did quite well until about 1730, when the Dutch finally lost their famous intermediary position on which their prosperity had rested. What did decline in Amsterdam was the Baltic grain trade. In the late sixteenth and early seventeenth centuries Amsterdammers played an important entrepreneurial role in importing grain from Poland and elsewhere in Eastern Europe and selling it in the Netherlands or re-exporting it to Italy, Spain and elsewhere. C.P. Hooft,* for example, had been involved in this trade. In 1631 the price of Prussian rye at Amsterdam reached its peak: 263 florins per last. Thereafter it sank, and wheat prices followed. This decline was counteracted by the rise of the East Indies trade, but the period 1650-70 was (to judge from the decline in income from the 'convoys and licences') a period of decline in Amsterdam trade as a whole. At this point Jan de Witt was making investment in the public debt an attractive proposition. Where the Venetian élite moved from trade into land, the Amsterdammers began to move from trade into bonds.[25]

These explanations are far from complete. In the case of Amsterdam, it is also necessary (for example) to take into account the rise in the amount of business transacted in the Town Council; to be a regent was becoming more of a full-time job, incompatible with an active interest in trade. If rulers need to have charisma, then one might say that the use of titles by the Amsterdam élite and their more gentlemanly style of life had a political function; the unheroic bourgeois had to turn gentleman to be obeyed.[26]

There is also the problem of relating changes of attitude within families to changes within groups. This problem is a slight one in Venice, where the proctors of 1720 were drawn from more or less the same clans as the proctors of 1580. It is a much greater one in Amsterdam, where new families entered the city and the élite in the course of the seventeenth century. But the problem has a solution; the link between changes in the attitudes of specific families and in the élite as a whole is a demographic one.

In seventeenth-century Europe there was not only economic stagnation but a halt in the growth of population. There was in fact a vicious circle because hard times led to increased celibacy and later marriage (couples could not afford to marry), but these reinforced population decline which made times harder (because demand for products then decreased).[27] This demographic decline hit Amsterdam late because immigration as well as natural increase had been pushing up her population. From 1580 to 1680 there was continuous immigration to Amsterdam, including men with capital, skills and ambition. A number of these immigrants, as we have seen, entered the élite, and in other cases their sons did. This continued immigration was (I should like to suggest) the reason for the survival of entrepreneur attitudes in Amsterdam. When the process of 'aristocratisation' pushed the de Graeffs, for example, out of trade, other families, like the Graaflands, came to take their place. But about 1680 Amsterdam stopped growing. The frontier closed at last. After 1672, when two were inserted by the Prince of Orange, only one first-generation immigrant entered the Amsterdam élite, which naturally became predominantly rentier in composition.

The Republics of Venice and the United Provinces continued to exist until the end of the eighteenth century, but from the point of view of the social historian, a cycle of important changes had been completed by about the year 1720.

1 The patricians at play: nobles fowling on the Venetian lagoons, armed with guns and *archi da balle* — bows loaded with terracotta pellets.

2 Amsterdam informality: B. Van de Helst's portrait of Daniel Bernard,* 1626-1714, for twenty-seven years a member of the Town Council. The spire in the background is that of the Bourse, and there are East India Company documents on the table.

Within the image, top left caption: *Chiesa del Rede Pintore di Capuzzi*

Within the image, bottom right: *Franco Forma con Priuilegio*

3 Venetian formality: proctor in official robes.

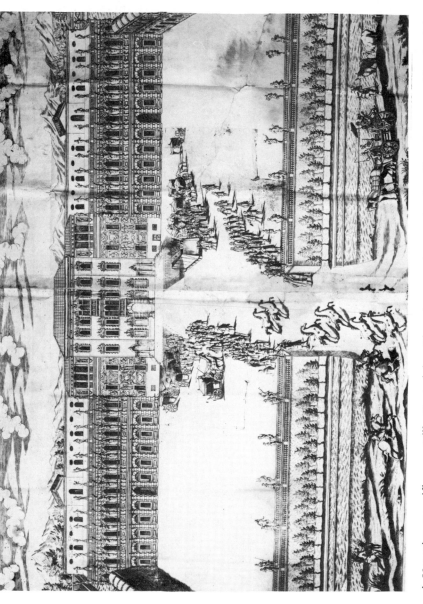

4 Venetian magnificence: Villa Contarini at Piazzola, a good example of a villa-palace, owned by the rich, art-loving Marco Contarini,* 1631-89.

5 Amsterdam
simplicity: Gunterstein
on the Vecht, a villa
owned by Ferdinand
van Collen,*
1651-1735.

6 Church of S. Moisè, Venice. A flamboyant piece of baroque architecture and sculpture, commissioned by Vincenzo Fini,* one of the few parvenus in the Venetian elite.

7 The Town Hall of Amsterdam. The monumental simplicity of the design reflects Dutch bourgeois taste. The baroque sculpture in the pediments is rendered unobtrusive in this print.

8 Willem van Loon,* 1633-95, at the age of thirty months. He became burgomaster fifty years later. The existence of the portrait suggests that parents in this social group were interested in their children as individuals; the child's costume suggests that even the under-sevens were seen as little adults.

Appendix
The investments of the Amsterdam élite

In the early 17th century

The property of J. P. Reael,* who died in 1621, was broken down as follows: 46% cash; 28% in houses; 12% in stock or voyages; 8% in bonds(including a private loan); 6% in land (Amsterdam, GA, Weeskamer, Div. Mem. vol. 3, folio 110).

Jacob Poppen,* who died in 1624, had about 55% of his wealth invested in land; 33% in bonds; 11% in houses (W. van Ravesteyn, *Onderzoeking over de ontwikkeling van Amsterdam* (Amsterdam, 1906, 331f.).

Barthold Cromhout* died in 1624, leaving just over 50% of his wealth invested in land (Ravesteyn, 276f.).

Jan Bal* (alias Huydecoper) died in 1624, leaving 66% of his wealth invested in houses; 24% in land; 10% in bonds (Amsterdam, GA, Weeskamer, Div. Mem. vol. 3, folio 212).

Simon de Rijck* died in 1652, leaving over 70% of his wealth invested in houses, and 25% in land (Amsterdam, GA, Registers of Collateral Succession, vol. 1, folio 1).

Cornelis Backer* declared his property at his marriage in 1655: 56% land and 44% bonds (Amsterdam, GA, Backer Papers, no. 77).

In the early 18th century

Fifteen members of the élite died childless between 1701 and 1725 and a breakdown of their wealth is therefore recorded in the Registers of Collateral Succession, now in the GA at Amsterdam.

Name	Date	Stock	Bonds	Houses	Land
A. Backer*	1701	—	41	55	4
D. Munter*	1701	50	12	20	18
C. Collen*	1704	60	40	—	—
J. Hudde*	1704	20	69	7	4
J. de Vries*	1708	23	62	9	6
F. W. van Loon*	1708	—	70	—	30

Name	Date	Stock	Bonds	Houses	Land
D. Bas*	1709	—	76	23	1
J. Bicker*	1713	1	95	—	4
D. Bernard*	1714	26	59	9	6
N. Witsen*	1717	10	80	5	5
J. Blocquery*	1719	71	14	15	—
A. Velters*	1719	68	25	7	0.3
N. Bambeeck*	1722	64	33	—	3
M. van Loon*	1723	9	58	22	11
J. de Haze*	1725	77	15	6	2

(all figures expressed in percentages)

Acknowledgements

The research in Venice and Amsterdam necessary for this book was made possible by the Leverhulme Trust which made me a Faculty Fellow in European Studies in 1972. I am most grateful to the Trust. I should also like to thank the staff of the Archivio di Stato at Venice and the Gemeente Archief at Amsterdam, in particular Dr F. Tiepolo and Dr S. Hart. For advice, information and encouragement I am grateful to Dr Gaetano Cozzi, of Venice (whose publications are cited so frequently in this book); Dr Brian Pullan, of Manchester; Professor K. Swart, of London; Professor I. Schöffer, of Leyden; Professor C. H. Wilson, of Cambridge, and to Riccardo Steiner. Teaching a course at the University of Sussex on 'aristocracies and élites' led me to the subject in the first place, and discussions with the students taking it did a great deal to clarify my ideas, as did conversations with fellow-workers in Venice—Bill Brown, Alex Cowan, Oliver Logan, Ed Muir and Jim Williamson. Parts of this book in draft form have been tried out on audiences at the Universities of Edinburgh and London, and at the Royal Historical Society's conference on 'Urban Civilization' at Oxford in 1972. A number of the suggestions made on these occasions proved most helpful. For their careful scrutiny of the typescript and for the improvements they suggested, I should like to thank Professor John Hale, Rupert Wilkinson and Maurice Temple Smith.

For permission to reproduce the photographs the author and publisher would like to thank the British Museum (plates 1 and 3); Museum Boymans van Beuningen, Rotterdam (plate 2); Museo Correr, Venice (plate 4); Rijksdienst v.d. Monumentenzorg, The Hague (plate 5); Fotokommissie, Rijksmuseum, Amsterdam (plate 8); the Mansell Collection (plates 6 and 7).

Bibliography

This bibliography is restricted to the most important secondary sources. For further information, see the notes to each chapter.

To my knowledge only two books deal with Amsterdam and Venice together: H. Havard, *Amsterdam et Venise* (Paris 1876), a travel book, and J.C. de Jonge, *Nederland en Venetië* (The Hague 1852), a study of the relations between the two states.

Outstanding studies of two members of the élite and their milieu are G. Cozzi, *Il doge Nicolò Contarini* (Venice/Rome 1958), and H.A. Enno van Gelder, *De Levensbeschouwing van C.P. Hooft* (Amsterdam 1918).

On the structure of the Amsterdam élite, the indispensable book is J.E. Elias, *De Vroedschap van Amsterdam*, 2 vols (Haarlem 1903-5). H. van Dijk and D.J. Roorda, 'Sociale mobiliteit onder regenten van de Republiek', *Tijdschrift voor Geschiedenis* (1971), is a quantitative and comparative study of the regents of Amsterdam, Zierikzee and Veere. For a more general survey see D.J. Roorda, 'The ruling class in Holland in the seventeenth century', in J.S. Bromley and E.H. Kossmann (eds.) *Britain and the Netherlands*, vol.2 (Groningen 1964). On the Dutch social structure, I. Schöffer, 'La stratification sociale de la République des Provinces-Unies au XVIIe siècle', in R. Mousnier (ed.), *Problèmes de stratification sociale* (Paris 1968). On the Dutch family, A.M. van der Woude, in P. Laslett (ed.), *Household and family in past time* (Cambridge 1972).

On the structure of the Venetian élite, there are biographies of the doges in A. da Mosto, *I dogi di Venezia*, second edn, (Milan 1960), but nothing in print on the proctors as a group. On the Venetian nobility as a whole, E. Rodenwalt, 'Untersuchungen über die Biologie des Venezianisches Adels', *Homo*, vol. 8 (1957); J.C. Davis, *The Decline of the Venetian Nobility as a Ruling Class* (Baltimore 1962).

On Amsterdam politics, J.E. Elias, *Geschiedenis van het Amsterdamsche Regentenpatriciaat* (The Hague 1923) (a revised version of the introduction to his *Vroedschap*); G.W. Kernkamp, 'Historie en regeering', in A. Bredius (ed.), *Amsterdam in de 17e eeuw*, 3 vols (The Hague 1897), and also his review of Elias, 'Amsterdamsche patriciërs', *Vragen des Tijds* (1905). On the institutions of the United Provinces, S.J. Fockema Andreae, *De Nederlanse Staat onder de Republiek* (Amsterdam 1961). J.G. van Dillen, 'Amsterdam's role in seventeenth century Dutch politics and its economic background' in J.S. Bromley and E.H. Kossmann (eds), *Britain and the Netherlands*, vol. 2 (Groningen 1964).

On Venetian politics, a useful narrative account is S. Romanin, *Storia documentata di Venezia*, vol. 7 (Venice 1858). Venetian political institutions are discussed by G. Maranini, *La constituzione di Venezia* (Venice 1931). On the Interdict crisis and its background, W.J. Bouwsma, *Venice and the Defense of Republican Liberty* (Berkeley and Los Angeles 1968). On the navy, M. Nani Mocenigo, *Storia della marina veneziana* (Rome 1935). On offices and their holders, J.C. Davis, *op.cit.*, and B. Pullan, 'Service to the Venetian state' in *Studi Secenteschi* (1964). The best guide to Venetian politics in the early seventeenth century remains Cozzi's study of Nicolò Contarini.

On the economic basis of the Amsterdam élite, H. Brugmans, 'Handel en nijverheid' in A. Bredius (ed.), *Amsterdam in de 17e eeuw*, 3 vols (The Hague 1897-); W. van Ravesteyn, *Onderzoeking over de ontwikkeling van Amsterdam* (Amsterdam 1906) (which stops about 1625); V. Barbour, *Capitalism in Amsterdam in the Seventeenth Century* (Baltimore 1950). On property development, N. de Roever, 'Tweeërlei regenten' *Oud-Holland* 7 (1889). On the VOC, J.G. van Dillen's introduction to its *Aandeelhoudersregister* (register of shareholders) (The Hague 1958); on the West India Company, W.J. van Hoboken, 'The Dutch West India Company', in J.S. Bromley and E. H. Kossman (eds), *Britain and the Netherlands*, vol. 1 (London 1960); J.G. van Dillen, 'De West-Indisch Compagnie, het Calvinisme en de politiek', *Tijdschrift voor Geschiedenis* 74 (1961).

On Venice, D. Beltrami, *Forze di lavoro e proprietà fondiaria nelle campagne venete* (Venice/Rome 1961), deals with economic penetration of the mainland; A. Stella, 'La crisi economica veneziana della seconda metà del secolo XVI', in *Archivio Veneto* (1956), deals with the shift from trade to land. S.J. Woolf, 'Venice and the terraferma', in B. Pullan (ed.), *Crisis and Change in the Venetian Economy* (London 1968), is a critical discussion of Beltrami. The same volume contains D. Sella, 'Crisis and transformation in Venetian trade'. See also U. Tucci, 'The psychology of the Venetian merchant in the sixteenth century', and B. Pullan, 'The occupations and investments of the Venetian nobility in the middle and late sixteenth century', in J.R. Hale (ed.), *Renaissance Venice* (London 1973). Other important studies of agriculture are J. Georgelin, 'Une grande propriété en Vénitie au 18e siècle', in *Annales E.S.C.* (1968), and A. Ventura, 'Considerazioni sull' agricoltura veneta', *Studi storici* (1968).

On Amsterdam culture, K. Fremantle, *The Baroque Town Hall of Amsterdam* (Utrecht 1959), is wider in scope than the title implies. R.B. Evenhuis, *Ook dat was Amsterdam*, 2 vols, (Amsterdam 1965-7), deals with religion from a Calvinist point of view. On the Arminian dispute, C. Bangs, 'Dutch theology, trade and war' in *Church History*

(1970), R. van Luttervelt, *De buitenplaatsen aan de Vecht*, section 1 (1943), deals with country houses in a region where there were many Amsterdam owners.

On Venetian culture, F. Haskell, *Patrons and Painters* (London 1963), focuses on the eighteenth century but has something to say about the seventeenth; S. Savini-Branca, *Il collezionismo veneziano nel '600*, (Padua 1964), deals with art collecting; W.J. Bouwsma, *op. cit.*, discusses patrician attitudes; a general study of Venetian cultural history of the period is P. Molmenti, *La storia di Venezia nella vita privata*, English trans. of the relevant volume (London 1908).

NOTES

Abbreviations

ASV Archivio di Stato, Venice

Bollettino Bollettino di storia della società e dello stato veneziano (now renamed Studi Veneziani)

EIP Esame istorico politico (anonymous ms. in Venice, Biblioteca Correr, Gradenigo 15)

GA Gemeente Archief, Amsterdam

RA 'Relazione dell'anonimo', ed. P. Molmenti in his *Curiosità di storia Veneziana*, (Bologna 1919)

BMV Biblioteca Marciana, Venice

BCV Biblioteca Correr, Venice

The Study of Élites (page 9)

1 G.M. Trevelyan, *English Social History* (London 1942) p. vii. For a good brief account of the value of comparative history, see F. Redlich, 'Toward comparative historiography', *Kyklos* XI, 1958.

2 See epigraph.

3 The original formulation of the idea of two types of élite was in an article of 1911, 'Rentiers et spéculateurs'. But the best-known expression of it is in his *Trattato di sociologia generale* (Florence 1916), paragraph 2233 onwards. This numbering of paragraphs is preserved in English translations.

4 R.A. Dahl, 'A critique of the ruling élite model', *American Political Science Review*, 52 (1958).

5 I owe this criticism of Dahl to my friend and colleague Rupert Wilkinson.

6 R. A. Dahl, *Who Governs?* New Haven 1961.
7 Duc de Rohan, *Mémoires* (Paris 1661), vol. 2, p. 359, describes his impressions of Amsterdam in 1600 and the similarities to Venice: 'Je ne trouve rien en l'une qui n'ait beaucoup de conformité en l'autre.' P.J. Blok, (ed.), *Relazioni veneziane* (The Hague 1909), prints Donà's report; the quotation comes from p. 112. On the Amsterdam pamphlet, see chapter 3, note 32 below.
8 L. Stone, 'Prosopography', *Daedalus* (Winter 1971).
9 C. Yriarte, *Un patricien de Venise* (Paris 1885); G. Cozzi, *Il doge Nicolò Contarini* (Venice/Rome 1958); F. Seneca, *Leonardo Donà* (Padua 1959); H.A. Enno van Gelder, *De levensbeschouwing van C.P. Hooft* (Amsterdam 1918); J.F. Gebhard, *Het leven van Mr Nicolaas Witsen* (Utrecht 1881); C.W. Roldanus, *Coenraad van Beuningen* (The Hague 1931); H. Terpstra, *Jacob van Neck* (Amsterdam 1960).
10 Contrast the suggestions of R.B. Notestein, 'The Patrician', *International Journal of Comparative Sociology*, 9 (1968), for whom patricians are upper class office-holders of old family in a society where there are also non-patricians in office and in the upper class.

Structure (page 16)

No references will be given for biographical material drawn from the following three sources: J.E. Elias, *De vroedschap van Amsterdam*, 2 vols. (Haarlem 1903-5); *Il Barbaro*, annotated family trees of the Venetian nobility, in manuscript, compiled in the seventeenth and eighteenth century, copies in the BCV and the ASV; G.A. Capellari, *Il campidoglio veneto*, an early-eighteenth-century manuscript with notes on Venetian nobles, now in the BMV (It. VII. 8304).
1 For a useful discussion of the difference between 'Estates and Classes', see R. Mousnier, *Les hiérarchies Sociales* (Paris 1969), chapters 1 and 3.
2 The nobles in 1594 are listed in a manuscript in the BCV Donà 225; the nobles in 1719, in BCV Cicogna 913. The population of Venice was about 135,000 in 1581; fell to 102,000 in 1633, following the plague; had climbed back to 138,000 in 1696 (D. Beltrami, *Storia della populazione di Venezia* [Padua 1954] p. 38).
3 The figure of 800 offices comes from J.C. Davis, *The Decline of the Venetian Nobility as a Ruling Class* (Baltimore 1962), p. 22. A possible approach to the problem of identifying possible key offices would be to computerize the information in the *Segretario alle voci* documents in the ASV and see what other offices are held by holders of known key offices.
4 On the tax records see chapter 4, note 1.

5 P. Molmenti (ed.), 'Relazione del'anonimo', in his *Curiosità di storia veneziana* (Bologna 1919), p. 401. Henceforth this source will be cited as RA.

6 A contemporary description of the proctors is F. Manfredi, *Degnità procuratoria di Venezia* (Venice 1602). Their duties are set out in the commissions issued to individual proctors; for example, that given to Alvise Barbarigo* in 1649 is preserved in the BCV Cicogna 2233. The seven doges who were not proctors were C. Contarini,* D. Contarini,* F. Corner,* B. Valier,* M.A. Zustinian,* Zuan II Corner* and Alvise II Mocenigo.* The proctors can be listed by consulting the *Segretario alle voci, elezioni del Maggior Consiglio*; there are also manuscript catalogues which cover the period in the BCV and in the BMV (both eighteenth-century compilations).

7 C.P. Hooft, *Memoriën en Adviesen*, I (Utrecht 1871), pp. 109, 168.

8 K. 8670, p. 2. That is, no. 8670 in W.P.C. Knuttel's catalogue of the pamphlets in the Royal Library in The Hague.

9 On *classis*, see the *Woordenboek der Nederlandsche Taal* (1892 onwards) under this term; Spinoza is quoted by S. Ossowski, *Class Structure in the Social Consciousness*, English trans. (London 1963), p. 122n.

10 Sir William Temple, *Observations upon the United Provinces*, ed. G. N. Clark (Cambridge 1932), p. 97.

11 Compare I. Schöffer, 'La stratification sociale de la République des Provinces-Unies au 17e siècle', in R. Mousnier (ed), *Problèmes de stratification sociale*, (Paris 1968).

12 Quoted in C. Wilson, *Queen Elizabeth and the Revolt of the Netherlands* (London 1970), p. 23. One member of the Amsterdam town council at this time, B. Appelman,* was indeed a dealer in cheese.

13 This point was made by Robert Fruin, 'Bijdrage tot de geschiedenis van het burgermeesterschap van Amsterdam tijdens de Republiek', in *Bijdragen voor Vaderlandsche Geschiedenis en Oudheidskunde*, Derde Reeks, V (1889).

14 Elias, *op. cit.*, biographies 1-305 inclusive, plus 14 burgomasters not councillors: in chronological order they are F. de Vrij,* J. de Vrij,* J. Backer,* J. Boelens,* F.H. Oetgens,* J. Cat,* G.J. Witsen,* H. Bicker,* C. Bicker,* A. van Bempden,* J. van den Poll,* C. van Bambeeck,* J. van Graafland,* J. Munter.*

15 On Amsterdam tax records, see chapter 4, note 27 below.

16 G. Contarini, *La republica e i magistrati di Vinezia* (Venice 1544), f. 58.

17 The idea of the 'tripod' comes from the anonymous seventeenth-century manuscript *Esame istorico politico* (henceforth EIP) in, BCV,

Gradenigo 15. The quotation from the anonymous seventeenth century manuscript *Relatione della città e republica di Venetia*, in the British Museum, Add. 10,130, f. 77 verso.

18 The phrase 'princes of the blood' from the anonymous seventeenth-century manuscript *Distinzioni segrete che corrono tra le casate nobili di Venezia*, in BMV. It. VII. 2226, p. 18. For the Corner as the 'Medici', Z.A. Venier (attributed), *Storia delle rivoluzioni seguite nel governo della Republica di Venezia*, manuscript in BCV Cicogna 3762 p. 137.

19 C. Freschot, *Nouvelle relation de la ville et république de Venise* (Utrecht 1709), p.263.

20 A. da Mosto, *I dogi di Venezia*, second edn, (Milan 1960), p. 314: EIP, p. 42.

21 RA, p. 401.

22 EIP, p. 63; RA, p. 401

23 EIP, 67f.

24 EIP, 77f.

25 Francesco da Molin, *Compendio*, manuscript in BMV. It. VII. 8812, p. 124.

26 On the population of Amsterdam, see P. Schraa, 'Onderzoekingen naar de bevolkingsomvang van Amsterdam 1550-1650', *Jaarboek Amstelodanum* 46 (1954).

27 J.G. van Dillen (ed.), *Bronnen tot de geschiedenis van het bedrijfsleven en het gildwesen van Amsterdam*, I (The Hague 1929), p. xxxii.

28 J.E. Elias, *Geschiedenis van het Amsterdamsche Regentenpatriciaat* (The Hague 1923), p. 119.

29 ibid., p. 105.

30 N. Witsen, 'Kort verhael van mijn levensloop', in P. Scheltema (ed.), *Aemstel's Oudheid* 6 (1872) p. 43.

31 S. Muller, *Schetsen uit de middleeuwen* 2 (Amsterdam 1914), 369f.

32 For the list of nobles in 1594, see note 1 above.

33 G. Cozzi, *Il doge Nicolò Contarini* (Venice/Rome 1958), p. 6n.

34 A. da Mosto *op. cit.*, p. 358.

35 P. Litta, *Celebri famiglie italiane* (Milan 1819-), vol. 2, genealogy of the Correr family; see Elisabetta Correr (d. 1706).

36 RA, pp. 374, 395.

37 Antonio Grimani's* will (1624). Here and hereafter I give no references for wills preserved in the ASV and entered on the card-index of wills accessible there.

38 BMV, manuscript Gradenigo Dolfin, 134, p. 138.

39 Beltrami, *op. cit.*, 188f.

40 G. Gualdo Priorato, *Sceno d'alcuni uomini illustri*, vol. 2, (Venice 1659), biography ot 'Giovanni Delfino'.

41   These are the figures put forward by E. Rodenwalt, 'Untersuchungen über die Biologie des venezianischen Adels' *Homo* 8 (1957), based on his sample of 21 Venetian families. Thanks to his work and that of J.C. Davis *op. cit.*, I treat demographic problems of the Venetian nobility in a relatively summary fashion.

42   For a general survey of Dutch family structure, see A.M. van der Woude, 'De omvang en samenstelling van de huishouding in Nederland in het verleden', in *Afdeling Agrarische Geschiedenis, Bijdragen* 15 (1970): English version in P. Laslett (ed.) *Household and Family in Past Time* (Cambridge 1972).

43   See G.J. Renier, *The Dutch Nation* (London 1944), ch. 9.

Political functions   (page 33)

1   D. Beltrami, *Storia della popolazione di Venezia* (Padua 1954), 63f.

2   As the *Segretario alle voce* records were not available when I was in Venice, I have had to rely on Barbaro and Capellari (above, p. 119) for details about offices. As important offices only are the subject of enquiry, they are probably reliable; but the figures quoted in the text should not be taken as more than approximate.

3   For details on the navy, see M. Nani Mocenigo, *Storia della marina veneziana* (Rome 1935); for the land forces, Professor John Hale's forthcoming book (which will go up to 1630) will fill a serious gap.

4   F. Nani Mocenigo, *A. Nani* (Venice 1894), p. 100.

5   G. Cozzi, *Il doge Nicolò Contarini* (Venice/Rome 1958), p. 149f.

6   J. C. Davis, *The Decline of the Venetian Nobility as a Ruling Class* (Baltimore 1962), ch. 1, is an important discussion of the structure of politics in Venice, as is B. Pullan, 'Service to the state' in *Studi Secenteschi* (1964), who disagrees with Davis in important respects.

7   G. Contarini, *La republica e i magistrati di Venezia* (Venice 1544); T. Boccalini, *Ragguagli di Parnasso*. 3 vols. (Bari 1910-48).

8   J. Bodin, *Six Livres de la République*, Book 4, ch. 1 (I quote the 1606 translation by R. Knolles); G. Bacco (ed), *Relazione sulla organizzazione politica della Repubblica di Venezia al cadere del secolo xvii* (Vicenza 1856).

9   F. da Molin *Compendio*, manuscript in BMV, It. VII. 8812, p. 119. Molin is one of the writers who refer to conflicts between 'youngsters' and 'old men' in Venetian politics in the late sixteenth century, conflicts central to the studies by G. Cozzi (above, note 5) and W.J. Bouwsma, *Venice and the Defense of Republican Liberty* (Berkeley and Los Angeles 1968). For a more sceptical approach, see M. J. C. Lowry, 'The reform of

the Council of X, 1582-3', in *Studi Veneziani* XIII (1972). Lowry warns historians against taking youngsters and old men as organized groups.

10 Bacco, *op. cit.,* p. 35.

11 On R. Zen,* see especially the chapter in Cozzi, *op. cit.*

12 Z.A. Venier, (attributed) *Storia delle rivoluzioni seguite nel governo della Republica di Venezia,* manuscript in BCV, Cicogna 3762, p. 119; see also Cozzi, *op. cit.,* 247n.

13 I take this suggestion from M. Gluckman, *Custom and Conflict in Africa* (Oxford 1956), ch. 1.

14 On the secretaries in 1582, da Molin, *op. cit.,* p. 119f; on the secretaries and the Zen movement, Cozzi, *op. cit.,* p. 265f.

15 Botero's point is developed in B. Pullan, *Rich and Poor in Renaissance Venice* (Oxford 1971), p. 626.

16 On the *Bestia di molti capi,* see the anonymous *Relatione del politico governo di Venezia* (1620) in the British Museum, Add. Mss. 18,660, f. 139 verso. On the political function of the fist-fights, another anonymous work in the British Museum, *Relatione della città e republica di Venezia,* in Add. Mss. 10, 130, f. 77 verso.

17 G. Botero, *Relatione della repubblica venetiana* (Venice 1595), p. 43f.

18 About 30 of the 100 families who joined the Venetian nobility in the period were noble families from the mainland. See C. Freschot, *Nouvelle relation de la ville et république de Venise* (Utrecht 1709), para 3 and ASV, Misc. Cod. III, Cod. Soranzo 15. These two authors usually but not always agree on the origin of specific families.

19 B. Pullan, (*op. cit.*) stresses that the *rettori* often 'found themselves helpless before the complexities of local intrigue'. The example quoted comes from B. Belotti, *Storia di Bergamo,* vol. 4 (Bergamo 1959), p. 54.

20 On Erizzo, Add. Mss. 10,130 (as note 16 above), f. 84 verso. Zagallo, quoted by N. Borgherini-Scarabellin, *La vita private a Padova nel secolo XVII* (Venice 1917), p. 42. P. Sarpi (attributed) *Opinione toccante il governo della Republica Veneziana* (London 1788); I quote from the English version (London 1707), p. 55. One has to allow for the possibility that this advice is a satire on the Venetians. A. Ventura, *Nobiltà e popolo nella società veneta del '400 e '500* (Bari 1964), p. 385, 469f., discusses the Venetian *rettori* as mediators between the nobles and the people of the mainland.

21 D.J. Roorda, *Partij en Factie* (Groningen 1961), p. 70f.

22 It is curious that Johan Huizinga, in his classic study of the play element in culture, *Homo Ludens* (1938), English trans. (London 1941), does not mention the *schutterij,* though Huizinga knew a great deal about the Dutch Republic in the seventeenth century.

23 J. E. Elias, *Geschiedenis van het Amsterdamsche Regentenpatriciaat* (The Hague 1923), p. 202.

24   K. 6773, p. 4: that is, *Den Ommegang van Amsterdam*, no. 6773 in W.P.C. Knuttel's catalogue of the pamphlets in the Royal Library in The Hague.

25   G. Schaep,* 'Alloquium ad filios' (1655), in *Bijdragen en Mededelingen van de Historische Genootschap* 16 (1895), p. 356f.

26   Amsterdam, GA, Vroedschap, Resolutiën, vols. for 1700-1702. J.G. van Dillen once compared Amsterdam with Venice as rare examples of seventeenth-century town councils discussing international affairs: 'Amsterdam's role in seventeenth-century Dutch politics', in J.S. Bromley and E.H. Kossmann (eds.), *Britain and the Netherlands,* vol. 2 (Groningen 1964), p. 147.

27   For a good general discussion, P. Geyl, *The Netherlands in the 17th century,* vol. 1, English trans. (London 1961), ch. 2; for the institutional background, S.J. Fockema Andreae, *De Nederlanse Staat onder de Republiek* (Amsterdam 1961). Compare H. Rowen, 'Jan de Witt' in *Société Jean Bodin Gouvernés et Gouvernants* (Brussels 1966).

28   C.P. Hooft, *Memorien en Adviezen,* I (Utrecht 1871), p. 70. For an account of the activities of one of the élite in the Raad van State, see H. Terpstra, *Jacob van Neck* (Amsterdam 1950), pp. 138f. 165f.

29   On the VOC, see J.G. van Dillen's introduction to his edition of the first register of shareholders (The Hague 1958); on the WIC, W.J. van Hoboken, 'The Dutch WIC', in Bromley and Kossman, *op. cit.,* vol. I, (London 1960); partly answered by J.G. van Dillen, 'De WIC, het calvinisme en de politiek', in *Tijdschrift voor Geschiedenis,* 74 (1961).

30   W.S. Unger, 'Het inschrijvings-register van de kamer Zeeland der VOC', *Economisch-Historisch Jaarboek,* vol. 24

31   M.A. van Rhede van der Kloot, *De gouverneurs-generaal ... van Nederlands Indië* (The Hague 1891).

32   K. 6773, 5-6 (see note 24 above).

33   J.H. Kernkamp, *De Handel op den Vijand,* vol. 2 (Utrecht n.d.), p. 190f.

34   H. Brugmans, 'Handel en Nijverheid', in A. Bredius (ed.), *Amsterdam,* vol. 2 (Amsterdam 1901), p. 61.

35   Elias, *op. cit.,* p. 79f.

36   ibid, p. 112f.

37   ibid, p. 173f.

38   Roorda, *op. cit.,* ch. 1, objects to the modern distinction between 'party' and 'faction' because the terms were used as synonyms by contemporaries (this goes for Italian as well as Dutch). All the same, it is convenient to have two terms for two kinds of group, and to reserve the term 'party' for a political group which is relatively highly organized, permanent and concerned with policies as well as personalities. Compare

R.W. Nicholson, 'Factions', in M. Barton (ed.), *Political systems and the Distribution of Power* (London 1965).
39 This point made by N. de Roever, 'Tweeërlei regenten', *Oud-Holland*, 7 (1889).
40 Compare R.A. Dahl, *Who governs?* (discussed in chapter 1 above) with his stress on decisions about urban redevelopment as a key area for discovering the distribution of power.
41 See below pp. 60f. (economic basis) and pp. 81f. (religion).
42 Amsterdam, GA, J. Hudde, *Brieven en papieren*, no. 42.

Economic Base (page 48)

1. The tax-returns are described by B. Canal, 'Il collegio, l'ufficio e l'archivio dei dieci savi', *Nuovo Archivio Veneto*, 16 (1908); J.C. Davis, *The Decline of the Venetian Nobility as a Ruling Class* (Baltimore 1962), writes them off (too easily, to my mind) as 'too sporadic' and 'difficult to consult'.
2 The tax-returns consulted for 1581 were those of M.A. Barbaro,* Ferigo Contarini,* Lorenzo Correr,* Andrea Dolfin,* Giacomo Foscarini,* Marco Grimani,* Andrea da Lezze,* Battista Morosini,* Vicenzo Morosini,* Gerolamo da Mula,* Paolo Nani,* Nicolò da Ponte senior* (the doge), Nicolò da Ponte junior,* Francesco Priuli,* Jacopo Soranzo,* Alvise Tiepolo,* Polo Tiepolo,* Nicolo Venier.*
The tax-returns consulted for 1711 were those of Polo Antonio Belegno,* Filippo Bon,* Pietro Bragadin,* Gerolamo Canal,* Alvise Contarini,* Carlo Contarini,* Pietro Contarini,* Francesco Corner,* Zuan Corner,* Nicolò Corner,* Vittore Correr,* Anzolo Diedo,* Daniel Dolfin,* Daniel Dolfin* (together), Vincenzo Fini,* Alvise Foscarini,* Giulio Giustinian,* Girolamo Giustinian,* Vincenzo Gradenigo,* Bortolo Gradenigo (three brothers of the name, together), Alvise Gritti,* Andrea da Lezze,* Francesco Loredan,* Girolamo Mocenigo,* Alvise Pisani,* Pietro Pisani, Polo Querini,* Carlo Ruzzini,* Nicolò Sagredo,* the brothers Andrea, Sebastian and Lorenzo Soranzo* (together), Lorenzo Tiepolo,* Girolamo Venier,* Piero Zen,* and Gabriel Zorzi.*
These returns have been microfilmed and deposited in the library of the University of Sussex, together with the exact references to the manuscript.
I also examined the tax-returns of Doge Domenico Contarini* and of twelve of the proctors in 1661, but have made little use of that information here. Detailed analysis of all these returns is complicated by the fact that much of the income declared is in kind, and it is not always clear

by what means the clerks arrived at the total from which tax was deducted. However, they do present a detailed picture of the kinds of property owned by Venetian patricians in the period.

3   Giacomo Agostinetti, *110 ricordi che formano il buon fattor di villa* (1679) (Venice 1704), pp. 58f., recommends a five-year lease. A three- to five-year lease was apparently the dominant system in the Padua area.

4   It is difficult to know what to allow for inflation, because studies of prices in the Veneto in the seventeenth century are lacking. Florentine and Lombard material suggests that prices doubled 1550-1600 but fell slightly 1600-1617 (C.M. Cipolla, 'The so-called "Price Revolution" ' in P. Burke [ed.], *Economy and Society in Early Modern Europe* [London 1972] , p. 44). Maddalena's researches on Milan and Parenti's on Siena suggest that the decline in prices became steeper in the 1630s and continued to the end of the century. An important discussion of these results is J. Meuvret, 'L'example des prix milanais', *Annales* E.S.C. (1953), criticized by R. Baehrel in the same journal for 1954; Baehrel argues that Italian prices began to fall at the end of the sixteenth century. F. Braudel, 'Note sull'economia del Mediterraneo nel 17 secolo', *Economia e storia* 2 (1955), notes a long-term recession in the Mediterranean world from about 1640 on. The trend seems clear, although its speed and the extent of regional variation are uncertain.

5   See the table in B. Pullan, 'Wage-earners in the Venetian economy, 1550-1630', in Pullan (ed.) *Crisis and Change in the Venetian Economy* (London 1968), p. 158.

6   On loans disguised as leases, see Pullan, 'The occupations and investments of the Venetian nobility in the middle and late sixteenth century', in J.R. Hale (ed.), *Renaissance Venice* (London 1973).

7   There is considerable need for a study of seventeenth-century Venetian investments which would explain the alternatives open to men with money, and gloss the technical terms used in the documents, like the 'matured shares' (*rate maturate*) referred to by Ferigo Corner* in 1708. Dr Brian Pullan suggested to me that they might be something like a deferred annuity.

8   I. Cervelli, 'Intorno alla decadenza di Venezia', *Nuova Rivista Storica*, 50 (1966), discusses A. Bragadin,* G. Foscarini* and their interest in the Venetian spice-trade. I owe the information about Zuanne Dolfin* and Agostino Nani* to the unpublished researches of Dr M.J.C. Lowry: 'The Church and Venetian political change in the later '500', Ph.D thesis (University of Warwick 1971), pp. 343, 354. On Almoro Tiepolo,* see ASV, Archivio Notarile, busta 720,f.181. I owe this reference to Alex Cowan.

9   Examples of dowries from 5,000 to 6,000 ducats: Zuan Barbarigo,*

Antonio Canal,* Domenico Contarini,* Francesco Corner,* 6,000 ducats was, in fact, the legal limit on dowries.

10   The ten cases are as follows: Molin*—Purperata (1576); Corner*—Noris (*c.* 1625); Soranzo*—Flangini (1640); Grimani*—Bergonzi (1646; the Bergonzi was ennobled in 1665); Foscarini*—Labia (1650; the Labia had been ennobled in 1646); Contarini*—Tomi (1665); Ottobon —Maretti (1665); Lando*—Zenobio (1668; the Zenobio family had been ennobled in 1647); Zen*—Pio (1692); Bragadin*—Zenobio (1697). It was also said that Doge Z. Pesaro married his housekeeper.

11   Campanella is quoted by A. Ventura, 'Considerazioni sull'agricoltura veneta', *Studi Storici* 9 (1968), p. 677.

12   On the Grimani, EIP, p. 47; on the Corner, A. Simioni, *Storia di Padova* (Padua 1968), p. 904; on the Dolfin, N.H.B.G. Dolfin, *I Dolfin* (Milan 1924), p. 163.

13   *Relatione di tutti le renditi e spese che la Repubblica di Venezia ordinariamente cava* . . ., British Museum, Add. Mss, 18,660 (anonymous, *c.* 1620),174f.

14   On 'alchemy', EIP, p. 18: on corruption in 1617, see the *Relatione del politico governo di Venezia*, anonymous (1620), bound in the same volume as the manuscript mentioned in note 12 above, f. 143 recto; on Morosini, A. da Mosto, *I dogi di Venezia*, second edn. (Milan 1960), p. 435.

15   G. Bacco (ed.), *Relazione sulla organizzazione politica della Repubblica di Venezia* (Vicenza 1856) (late seventeenth century), 153f. On the *bailo*, compare R.A. 393 and C. Freschot, *Nouvelle relation de la ville et république de* Venise (Utrecht 1709), p. 264.

16   F. Corner* in his will (1706), makes a bequest to 'my *fattore* in Venice. . . who knows about all my affairs'.

17   This information is from M.A. Barbaro's* tax-return of 1581, a document now in very bad condition.

18   ASV, Archivio Bernardo, Busta 22, *passim*, on Ferigo Contarini;* on Girolamo Corner* consult the card-index in BCV, Provenienze Diverse, under his name.

19   E. Campos, *I consorzi di bonifica nella repubblica veneta* (Padua 1937), especially pp. 15f. The approach followed is legal, and it is a pity that an economic historian does not study the same material.

20   BCV, Provenienze Diverse; see the card-index under 'Luca Michiel' for these and further examples.

21   *Relatione del politico governo di Venezia* (note 14 above), pp. 144f.

22   D. Beltrami, *Forze di lavoro e proprietà fondiaria* (Venice/Rome 1961), pp. 74f.

23   BCV, Provenienze Diverse, C. 2347, Busta 17.

24 On the *fattore*, see A. Ventura, 'Aspetti storico-economici della villa veneta', in *Bollettino Centro A. Palladio* XI (1969), and Giacomo Agostinetti, *op. cit.*

25 On Anguillara, J. Georgelin, in *Annales* (1968); the point about the absence of treatises on agriculture made by M. Berengo, *La società veneta alla fine del '700* (Florence 1956), p. 94.

26 G.B. Barpo, *Le delitie e i frutti dell'agricoltura e della villa* (Venice 1634), pp. 26f.

27 The *kohier* of 1585 has been edited by J.G. van Dillen (Amsterdam 1941); that of 1631 by J.G. Frederiks and P.J. Frederiks (Amsterdam 1890); that of 1742 by W.F.H. Oldewelt (Amsterdam 1945); that of 1674 remains unpublished in the GA at Amsterdam.

28 Hans Bontemantel, *De Regeering van Amsterdam*, (ed.) G.W. Kernkamp. (The Hague 1897) vol. 2, pp. 107f.

29 More particularly the Registers of Collateral Succession, which start in 1658; collateral heirs were subject to a 5 per cent tax on their inheritance, which had to be described in detail.

30 The 1622 estimate is quoted by G.W. Kernkamp in his chapter in A. Bredius (ed.) *Amsterdam in de 17de eeuw*, vol. I (The Hague 1897), p. 29; he does not give a reference.

31 Amsterdam, GA, Registers of Collateral Succession, vol. 19, f. 300.

32 ibid., vol. 16, f. 482.

33 ibid., vol. 13, f. 158.

34 Estimate of 1622, see note 30 above. The de Graeff papers are in the GA at Amsterdam. No. 43 contains the steward's accounts for the manor of Zuidpolsbroek 1555-1651, that is, when it was owned by a nobleman and when it was owned by one of the Amsterdam élite. It is well worth the attention of economic historians.

35 Amsterdam, GA, Backer papers, no. 63. On the importance of shares in voyages as a form of investment *c.* 1600, see H.A. Enno van Gelder, *De Levensbeschouwing van C.P. Hooft* (Amsterdam 1918), pp. 29f.

36 Amsterdam, GA, Registers of Collateral Succession, vol. 18, f. 1156.

37 ibid., vols. 18, f. 61 (Velters) and 19, f. 1017 (Haze).

38 Amsterdam, GA, Vroedschap, Resolutien, vol. 33, pp. 4f., gives the interest rate in 1679.

39 Contemporary occupational descriptions are conveniently compiled by J.E. Elias and included in the biographies in his *De Vroedschap van Amsterdam* (Haarlem 1903-5).

40 On the change about 1600, see Ravesteyn, *Onderzoekingen*, p. 272.

41 C. Koeman, *Joan Blaeu and his Grand Atlas* (Amsterdam 1970), p. 10.

42 A. Nielsen, *Danische Wirtschaftsgeschichte* (Jena 1933), pp. 141, 166.

43 J. Bouman, *Bedijking, opkomst en bloei van de Boemster,* (Purmerend 1856-7), pp. 263f.

44 Brugmáns (as chapter 3, note 34), p. 61.

45 N. de Roever, 'Tweeërlei regenten', *Oud-Holland* 7, (1889), pp. 66f.

46 After the foundation of the Amsterdam Exchange in 1609, it becomes relatively easy to convert ducats and florins. In 1609 the Venetian ducat was worth 106 *grooten* at Amsterdam. 1 *groot* was 0.025 of a florin, so the ducat exchanged for about 2½ florins. By 1718 the ducat had devalued to about 80 *grooten* or 2 florins (N.W. Posthumus, *Nederlandsche Prijsgeschiedenis* vol. I [Leyden 1943], pp. 590f.) The real problem is that of comparing Venetian income (derived from the *decima* of 1711) with Amsterdam property (derived from the *kohier* of 1674). (At a time of economic stagnation, the difference between these two dates does not have to be taken too seriously.) The comparison of income and property is a problem because property in Amsterdam could produce an income which varied between 3 per cent and 12 per cent a year. Somewhat arbitrarily I have chosen 5 per cent to convert Venetian income into Venetian property: 'twenty years' purchase', as English contemporaries would have called it.

47 Kernkamp, *op, cit.*, p. 100.

Style of Life (page 62)

1 Among other writers, Amelot de la Houssaie and Parival discuss the *moeurs* of the Venetians and the Amsterdammers respectively.

2 Poggio Bracciolini, *Facetiae* no. 21:I used the Paris 1880 edition; T. Coryat, *Crudities*, I (Glasgow 1905), p. 364: (Coryat visited Venice in 1608).

3 On Donà as a model noble, P. Sarpi, *Istoria dell'Interdetto*, (Bari 1940), p. 9: on Dona's thrift, A. Cutolo, 'Un diario inedito del doge Leonardo Dona', *Nuova Antologia* (1953), p. 278.

4 RA, p. 414.

5 Coryat, *op. cit.*, pp. 415, 397.

6 On sumptuary Laws see G. Bistort, *Il magistrato alle pompe nellea republica di Venezia* (Venice 1912, pp. 414-67 deal with the seventeenth century.

7 On Morosini,* A. da Mosto, *I dogi di Venezia*, second edn. (Milan

1960), p. 435; on N. Corner,* RA, p. 399; F. Moryson, *An Itinerary* I, (Glasgow 1907), p. 164.

8 Coryat, *op. cit.*, p. 399; M. Misson, *Nouvelle voyage d'Italie* (The Hague 1691), I, p. 196.

9 G. Bardi, *Dichiaratione di tutte le istorie* (Venice 1587), f. 30. On *taciturnità* F. Seneca, *Leonardo Donà* (Padua 1959), p. 37.

10 A. Colluraffi, *Il nobile veneto* (Venice 1623), p. 201. Amelot de la Houssaie, *Histoire du gouvernement de Venise* (Paris 1676), p. 338.

11 Donà quoted by W.J. Bouwsma, *Venice and the Defense of Republican Liberty* (Berkeley and Los Angeles 1968), p. 234.

12 For the terms *genio spagnuolo, genio francese*, see EIP, *passim*. On N. Corner,* RA, p. 399; on P. Dolfin,* RA, p. 374 and EIP, p. 49; on D. Contarini,* A. de St-Didier, *Venise* (Paris 1680), p. 180.

13 Riding academies spread on the mainland in the early seventeenth century. See J. Hale, 'Military academies on the Venetian *terraferma*', forthcoming in *Studi Veneziani.*

14 F. Erizzo* quoted by M. Borgherini-Scarabellin, *La vita privata a Padova nel secolo xvii* (Venice 1917), p. 12.

15 F.M. Piccioli, *L'Orologio del piacere* (Piazzola 1685), is the official account of proceedings.

16 M. Grimani's* expenses were printed by Giomo in *Archivio Veneto* (1887).

17 EIP, 63f.

18 RA, p. 391.

19 On N. Corner,* RA, p. 391; on Anzolo Contarini* and Renier Zen,* BCV Cicogna 2538.

20 Amsterdam, GA, Bicker Papers, no. 717.

21 H. Sidney, *Diary* I, (London 1843), pp. 63f.; Sir William Temple, *Observations upon the United Provinces*, (ed.) G.N. Clark, (Cambridge 1932), pp. 59f.

22 T. Contarini in P.J. Blok (ed.), *Relazioni veneziane* (The Hague 1909), p. 38.

23 RA, p. 384.

24 On the political market-place, Houssaie, *op. cit.*, p. 17, and St-Didier, *op. cit.*, p. 35.

25 On 'front', E. Goffman, *The presentation of self in everyday life*, (New York, 1959), pp. 22f.; Colluraffi, *op. cit.*, has a chapter on how the noble should behave at the broglio; the Malombra painting is referred to by C. Ridolfi, *Le Maraviglia'dell'arte* (Venice 1648), vol. 2, p. 157.

26 On Venetian academies, M. Battagia, *Delle accademie veneziane* (Venice 1826); on the Delphic Academy, F. Sansovino, *Venezia città nobilissima* (ed.) G. Martinioni (Venice 1663), p. 396

27 On the *Cacciatrice,* A Favaro, 'Un ridotto scientifico in Venezia al tempo di Galileo Galilei', *Nuovo Archivio Veneto* 5 (1893).
28 On the *Incogniti,* A. Lupis, *Vita di G. F. Loredano* (Venice 1663), p. 17; G.F. Loredan (ed.), *Discorsi academici* (Venice 1635); G.F. Loredan, *Bizzarrie accdemiche* (Bologna 1676).
29 F. Nani Mocenigo, *A. Nani* (Venice 1894), p. 164.
30 G. Sagredo,* *Arcadia in Brenta* (Venice 1669).
31 For fowling in the early seventeenth century, see Figure 3. Compare Longhi's drawing, *c.* 1750, in T. Pignatti, *Longhi* (London 1969), p. 101 and plate 180.
32 The importance of these villas in the past and the threat to them in the present were the themes of the exhibition in the Prinsenhof at Delft in 1972, *Nederlandse buitenplaatsen bedreigd?*
33 These houses were owned respectively by Willem Backer,* Nicolaes Witsen* and Andries de Graeff.*
34 J. van Heemskerk, *Batavische Arkadia.* Heemskerk was in fact the brother-in-law of Coenraed van Beuningen.* On Zesen, a German émigré, see J.H. Scholte, 'Philipp von Zesen', *Jaarboek Amstelodanum* 14 (1916). *De Zegepralende Vecht* was published in Amsterdam in 1719. It contains engravings of villas by Daniel Stopendaal and poems by Andries de Leth.
35 The volumes of 'resolutions' of the Town Council in the GA in Amsterdam show them meeting more and more rarely in June and August between 1650 and 1700.

Attitudes and Values   (page 71)

1 Figures calculated from P.A. Zeno, *Memoria de'scrittori veneti patritii* (Venice 1662), a list of books in alphabetical order of authors.
2 N. Contarini,* *De perfectione rerum* (Venice 1576); P. Paruta,* *Perfettione della vita politica* (Venice 1579); B. Nani,* *Historia della Republica Veneta* I (Venice 1662); G. Sagredo,* *L'Arcadia in Brenta* (Venice 1669), published under the pseudonym of 'Ginnesio Gavardo Vacalerio'; G. Sagredo,* *Memorie istoriche de' monarchi ottomani* (Venice 1673); all copies of da Ponte's* book seem to have disappeared, but Zeno, *op. cit.,* s.v. *Ponte,* claims it was published in 1585.
3 The poems of S. Contarini* and A. Ottobon* are in the Marciana Library in Venice. There are copies of N. Contarini's* history in the ASU; in the British Museum and elsewhere.
4 G. Cozzi, *Il doge Nicolo Contarini* (Venice/Rome 1958), p. 200n.
5 A. Colluraffi, *Il nobile Veneto* (Venice 1623); M. Boschini, *La Carta*

del navegar pitoresco. Dialogo. Tra un senator venetian deletante e un profesor di pitora.... I used the Venice 1660 edition.

6   G.F. Sagredo (brother of Zaccaria Sagredo*) to M. Welser 1614, quoted by W.J.Bouwsma, *Venice and the Defence of Republican Liberty* (Berkeley 1968), p. 87.

7   G. Sagredo,* *Arcadia in Brenta* (Venice 1669), p. 1.

8   A. Lupis, *Vita di G.F. Loredano* (Venice 1663), p. 25.

9   EIP, p. 34.

10   B. Castiglione, *Il Cortegiano* (Venice 1528) Book I, section 27.

11   On this distinction, see M.W. Croll, 'Attic prose in the 17th century', *Studies in Philology* (1921), reprinted in his *Style, Rhetoric and Rhythm* (Princeton 1966).

12   On official history, see G. Cozzi, 'Cultura politica e religione nella pubblica storiografia veneziana', *Bollettino* 5 (1965).

13   F. Seneca, *Leonardo Donà* (Padua 1959), p. 36.

14   See the inventory of the books and other possessions of F. Contarini* edited by M.T. Cipollato in the *Bollettino* 3 (1961).

15   Compare the points made by D. Chambers in his *The Imperial Age of Venice* (London 1970), pp. 12f.

16   A. Favaro, 'G.F. Sagredo e la vita scientifica in Venezia', *Nuovo Archivio Veneto* (1902).

17   Cozzi, *op. cit.*, p. 57; A.Tenenti, II *de perfectione rerum* di N. Contarini' *Bollettino* 1 (1959); A.Favaro, *Galileo Galilei e lo studio di Padova,* 2 vols, (Florence 1883), vol. 2, p. 74.

18   Favaro, *op. cit.*, vol. 2, p. 94, on Donà,* F. Sansovino, *Venezia città nobilissima,* (ed.) G. Martinioni, (Venice 1663), p. 371, on Z.B. Corner;* S. Romanin, *Storia documentata di Venezia,* vol. 7, (Venice 1858), p. 557, on B. Nani* and his academy.

19   Cipollato, *op. cit.*

20   A. Priuli's* memoirs are quoted in *Nuovo Archivio Veneto* (1891), p. 69.

21   *Dimettendo ad altri le sottili e troppo curiose investigationi*: Colluraffi, *op. cit.*, p. 56.

22   Favaro, *op. cit.*, vol. 2, p. 2 and document xci.

23   Bouwsma, *op. cit.*, stresses empiricism but perhaps plays down scholasticism too much; J.H. Randall Jr. *The School of Padua and the Emergence of Modern Science* (Padua 1961), says little about the period after 1600; L. Berthé de Besaucèle, *Les Cartésiens d'Italie* (Paris 1920), says little about Venice; B. Trevisan, *Meditazioni filosofiche* (Venice 1704); J. Addison, *Remarks on several parts of Italy* (London 1705), p. 84.

24   L. Reael,* *Observatien aen de magnetsteen* (Amsterdam 1651)

(posthumously published); N. Tulp,* *Observationes medicae*, (Amsterdam 1641); J. Commelin,* *Catalogus plantarum indigenarum Hollandiae*, (Amsterdam 1683); J. Blaeu,* *Geographia* (Amsterdam 1662); J. Six,* *Medea* (Amsterdam, 1648); C. van Beuningen,* *Alle de brieven ende schriften* (Amsterdam 1689); J. Hudde,* 'De reductione aequationum' and De 'maximis et minimis'. in R. Descartes, *Geometria*, (ed.) F. Schooten (Leyden 1659); N. Witsen,* *Scheepsbouw en bestier* (Amsterdam 1671); N. Witsen,* *Noord en Oast Tartarye*, second edn, (Amsterdam 1705). These are simply some of the most important books published by members of the élite; they are not an exhaustive list.

25 These books listed by H.A. Enno van Gelder, *De levensbeschouwing van C.P. Hooft* (Amsterdam 1918), appendix 2.

26 On Coster's* books see the 1594 inventory in Amsterdam, GA, Weeskamer, Boedelpapieren, Lade 139.

27 On this extraordinary man see A. Cameroni, *Uno scrittore avventuriero del secolo xvii* (s.l. 1893).

28 On Moses and Aaron, C.P. Hooft, *Memoriën en Adviesen* I (Utrecht 1871), p. 97. The plays referred to are P.C. Hooft, *Baeto* (Amsterdam 1626) and J. Vondel, *Batavische Gebroeders* (Amsterdam 1662).

29 *Fin de la Guerre*, no 3428 in Knuttel's catalogue of seventeenth-century pamphlets in the Royal Library in The Hague.

30 On the Town Hall, see K. Fremantle, *The baroque town hall of Amsterdam* (Utrecht 1959).

31 For Witsen's interests, see the books cited in note 24 above. The significance of Dr. Woodward's shield will be discussed by Professor J. Levine in a forthcoming book.

32 This side of Witsen* comes out clearly in the volume of documents published by J. Gebhard as the second volume of his biography, *Het leven van Mr Nicolaas Witsen* (Utrecht 1882).

33 A good short study of Hudde* by C. de Waard in *Nieuw Nederlands Biographical Woordenboek*, vol. I (Leyden 1911).

34 C.P. Hooft (as note 28), p. 206.

35 C.L. Thijssen-Schoutte, *Nederlands Cartesianisme* (Amsterdam 1954), pp. 246, 125f.

36 Van Gelder, *op. cit.,* especially part 2.

37 Amsterdam GA, Hudde, Brieven en Papieren, no. 49.

38 C.W. Roldanus, *Coenraad van Beuningen* (The Hague 1931).

39 This observation made by Philippe Canaye de Fresnes in 1604, quoted by Cozzi, *op. cit.*, p. 44. On Sarpi's ideas, see L. Salvatorelli, 'Le idee religiose di fra Paolo Sarpi', *Atti della Accademia Nazionale dei Lincei, Scienze Morali* (1953); G. Cozzi, 'Paolo Sarpi tra il cattolico Philippe

Canaye de Fresnes e il calvinista Isaac Casaubon' *Bollettino* I (1959); P. Burke (ed.), *Sarpi* (New York 1967); Bouwsma, *op. cit.*, especially the last three chapters.

40 Cozzi, *op. cit.*, pp. 211f.

41 F. Seneca, *Leonardo Donà* (Padua 1959), p. 36.

42 A. Stella, *Chiesa e stato nelle relazioni dei nunzi pontifici a Venezia* (Vatican City 1964), pp. 13f.; A. Stella, *Dall' anabattismo al socianesimo nel '500* (Padua 1967), p. 132.

43 Bouwsma, *op. cit.*, in his chapter 'Venice under the giovani' somewhat exaggerates the cohesiveness of this group. On the 'libertines' see G. Spini, *Ricerca dei libertini* (Rome 1950) who has a chapter on the circle of G.F. Loredan in Venice. No members of the élite seem to have been involved in charges of heresy or blasphemy, according to the inquisition records in the Archivio di Stato in Venice.

44 This story is told by Nicolò Contarini;* see Cozzi, *op. cit.*, p. 218.

45 G. Cozzi, 'Federico Contarini', *Bollettino* 3 (1961), especially pp. 196, 200.

46 G. Tiepolo, *Trattato delle santissime reliquie . . .* (Venice 1617).

47 All this material from wills which can be found in the card-index in the ASV.

48 The phrase is that of the *deputati alla fabrica* in 1679, quoted in G.A. Moschini, *La chiesa e il seminario di S. Maria della Salute* (Venice 1842), p. 27.

49 A good discussion of C.P. Hooft's religious views in part 2 of Van Gelder,*op. cit.* A brief account in English in J. Lecler, *Toleration and the Reformation* (London 1960), vol. 2, pp. 292f. A general discussion of Calvinism in Amsterdam is R.B. Evenhuis, *Ook dat was Amsterdam,* 2 vols (Amsterdam 1965-7); see vol. 1, p. 99 on R. Cant* and p. 275 on M. Coster.* Coster's* religious books are listed in an inventory of 1594 (above, note 26).

50 These Remonstrants are listed by G.W. Kernkamp in the introduction to his edition of H. Bontemantel,* *De Regeering van Amsterdam* (The Hague 1897), p. lxiv.

51 On the 'devout party', see J.E. Elias, *Geschiedenis van het Amsterdamsche Regentenpatriciaat* (The Hague 1932), 149f.; a good short study of R. Pauw* is that by W. van Ravesteyn in *Nieuw Nederlands d Biografische Woordenboek,* vol. 9 (Leyden 1911-37).

52 Amsterdam, GA, Bicker Papers, 717, 218-20.

53 On 'double puritans' see D. Carleton's report of a conversation with Oldenbarnevelt in 1617 in his *Letters* (London 1775), p. 100. For the views of G. Schaep see no. 717 of the Bicker Papers (note 52 above), *passim.*

54 Compare D.W. Howe, 'The decline of Calvinism', *Comparative*

Studies in Society and History 14 (1972); Howe also makes the point that in Boston, the move away from Calvinism by the upper middle class coincided with their shift from identification with the petty bourgeoisie to identification with the aristocracy. This may well have been true of Amsterdam too. On N. Witsen* see his *Moscovische Reyse* (eds. T.J.G. Locher and P. de Buck) 3 vols (The Hague 1966-7), especially pp. 400f., 455f; and his *Noord en Oost Tartarye*, 2nd edn. (Amsterdam 1705), pp. 664f.

55 On C. van Beuningen* see Roldanus, *op. cit.*, especially pp. 165f. On the Labadie movement, L. Kolakowski, *Chrétiens sans église* (Paris 1969).

Patronage of the Arts   (page 84)

1 On 'magnificence', P. Paruta,* *Della Perfezione della vita politica* (Venice 1579), p. 282: the speaker is Michele Surian. V. Scamozzi, *Idea dell'architettura universale* (Venice 1615), p. 243.

2 Besides wills, this paragraph depends on E. Bassi, *Architettura del '600 e del '700 a Venezia* (Naples 1968).

3 On villas the indispensable handbook is G. Mazzotti (ed.), *Le ville venete,* 2nd edn. (Treviso 1953).

4 On art-collecting, S. Savini-Branca, *Il collezionismo veneziano nel '600* (Padua 1964), is fundamental. The appendix includes descriptions of the collections of fifteen members of the élite.

5 A. Lupis, *Vita di GF Loredano*, Venice 1663, p. 41; C. Ivanovitch, *Minerva al tavolino* (Venice 1681), especially pp. 83, 103.

6 G. Cozzi,'Appunti sul teatro e i teatri a Venezia, agli inizi del '600', *Bollettino*, 5 (1965).

7 On the opera see S.T. Worsthorne, *Venetian Opera in the 17th century*, (Oxford 1954); T. Wiel, *I codici Musicali contariniani* (Venice 1888), catalogues 120 manuscripts from the Contarini collection. For a delightful description of a performance of an opera about Caesar and Scipio in Venice, see J. Addison, *Remarks on several parts of Italy* (London 1705), pp. 97f.

8 On the Huydecoper* house, see P. Vingboons, *Gronden en afbeeldsels der voornaamste gebouwen* (Amsterdam, 1688), f. 2 recto. The houses of J. de Bisschop* and D. Bernard* were valued in 1623 and 1714 respectively.

9 J. Wagenaar, *Amsterdam*, vol. 1, (Amsterdam 1779), p. 103

10 R. van Luttervelt, *De buitenplaatsen aan de Vecht* (s.l. 1943), p. 128. On 'Vredenhof', Amsterdam, GA, de Graeff papers, 608, f. 82 recto.

11   Amsterdam, GA, Bicker Papers, 717, section 4, p. 99.
12   J. Vos, *Alle de gedichten* (Amsterdam 1726), pp. 380f. Much of this collection (323f. in this edition) is taken up with verse descriptions of the collections of prominent Amsterdammers, an apparently under-exploited source on seventeenth-century Dutch patronage.
13   On de Graeff's* collection, Amsterdam, De Graeff papers, no. 608. This includes the 1733 inventory of the possessions of Alida de Graeff, who inherited goods from Andries de Graeff* (though we cannot be certain whether a given item was originally his or not); folios 56f are especially relevant. Tulp's* protest is quoted by K. Fremantle, *The Baroque Town Hall of Amsterdam* (Utrecht 1959), p. 64; for Tulp* and Potter, see A. Houbraken, *De Groote Schouwburg*, vol. 2 (Maastricht 1944), p. 102. On Calvinism and landscape, A. Cuyper, *Calvinism* (London 1932) chapter: 'Calvinism and art.'
14   J.A. Worp, *Jan Vos* (Groningen 1879), pp. 11f. discusses Amsterdam patrician patronage. Vondel dedicated *King David in Ballingschap* to A. de Graeff;* his translations of *Oedipus Rex* and *Iphigenia in Tauris* to J. Huydecoper;* the Batavische Gebroeders to S. van Hoorn;* *King David Hersteld* to C. van Vlooswijk.* The Latin verses written for Willem Backer* are preserved in Amsterdam, GA, Backer Papers, 70.
15   G. Brandt, *Leven van Vondel* (ed. S. Leendert Jr) (Amsterdam 1932), p. 14. Brandt wrote from personal knowledge of Vondel.
16   On the Amsterdam theatre, a good short account in J.A. Worp, *Geschiedenis van het drama . . . in Nederland*, vol. 2 (Groningen 1908), pp. 99f. Compare G. Kalff, *Literatuur en tooneel te Amsterdam in de 17de éeuw*, (Haarlem 1895).
17   For general discussions of the relationships, see W. Weisbach, *Der Barock als Kunst der Gegenreformation* (Berlin 1921), and L. Wencelius, *L'esthetique de Calvin* (Paris 1937).
18   On the tastes of F. Contarini,* O. Logan, *Culture and Society in Venice 1470-1790* (London 1972), p. 192. Savini-Branca, *op. cit.*, is the obvious work of reference here: see the many references in her index under Tintoretto, Peranda, etc. The characterization of Peranda's style comes from Boschini's *Minere*, in the introduction (no pagination).
19   M. Boschini, *Carta del navegar pittoresco* (Venice 1660), p. 553.
20   On the taste for the exotic in seventeenth-century Venice, see G. Getto, 'Il romanzo veneto nell'età barocca, reprinted in his *Barocco in prosa e in poesia* (Milan 1969).
21   On the Senate and P. Basadonna,* RA, 386. On the *Salute*, G. A. Moschini, *La chiesa e il seminario di S. Maria della Salute* (Venice 1842), pp. 7f.
22   Houbraken *op. cit.*, vol. 3, p. 402.

23 *ibid.*, vol. 2, p. 18. On de Graeff* and Rembrandt, S. A. C. Dudok van Heel, 'Het maecenaat de Graeff en Rembrandt' *Amstelodanum Maandblad* (1969), pp. 150f., 149f.
24 C.W. Roldanus, *Coenraad van Beuningen* (The Hague 1931), p. 57n. P. Schaep's* anagram in Amsterdam, GA, Bicker Papers, 717, section 4, p. 222. Vos, *op. cit.*, p. 399.

Training (page 94)

1 Quoted by F. Seneca, *Leonardo Donà* (Padua 1959), p. 9.
2 A fundamental source on Venetian noble family life is Francesco Barbaro, *De re uxoria*. Although this treatise was written in the fifteenth century, it is likely that the attitudes expressed in it were those of at least the more traditional Venetians of the seventeenth century. Book 2, chapter 8 makes the conventional recommendation that mothers should suckle their children themselves but goes on to give advice on picking a wet-nurse. On weaning, O. Ferrarius, whose book on the diseases of children was published at Brescia, in Venetian territory, in 1577, warns parents that weaning after the age of two makes children 'late developers' (*tardiusculi*) as if this were a common practice.
3 Barbaro, Book 2, ch. 8, (I used the Paris 1513 edition); C. Freschot, *Nouvelle relation de la ville et république de Venise* (Utrecht 1709), p. 261: A. de St-Didier, *Venise* (Paris 1680), p. 302; compare P. Molmenti, *La storia di Venezia nella vita privata*, 4th edn, vol. 3, (Bergamo 1908), pp. 52f.
4 'The higher nobility'—Freschot *op. cit.*, p. 261.
5 On Donà,* Seneca, *op. cit.*, p. 9; on Contarini,* G. Cozzi, *Il doge Nicolò Contarini* (Venice/Rome 1958), p. 55.
6 L. Mabilleau, *C. Cremonini* (Paris 1881).
7 *Relatione del politico governo di Venezia* (1920), anonymous, in British Museum, Add. Mss, 18,660, f. 145 recto.
8 Compare Sir Dudley Carleton on the shift from travel for economic reasons to travel for social reasons, p. 103 below.
9 The phrase 'political novitiate' from A. Lupis, *Vita di G.F. Loredano* (Venice 1663), p. 14.
10 M. Nani Mocenigo, *Storia della Marina veneziana* (Rome 1935), p. 24.
11 J. de Parival, *Les delices dé la Hollande,* new edn (Amsterdam 1669), pp. 20, 25.
12 Compare Melanie Klein, *Our Adult World and its Roots in Infancy* (London 1960); I owe this reference to Riccardo Steiner.

13 E.S. Morgan, *The Puritan Family*, new ed. (New York 1966), ch. 3, 'Parents and children'. This study of New England in the seventeenth century seems to have no parallel for the Netherlands, but one may usefully look at Jacob Cats, *Wercken* (Amsterdam 1955), as an expression of common attitudes (his works had sold 55,000 copies by 1655); see particularly his poem *Marriage* (*Houwelick*) first published in 1624, especially the section on the woman as mother, which recommends teaching the children to fear God; Cats was a member of the regent class, but from Zeeland. Compare the papers of two leading members of the devout faction, P. Schaep* and W. Backer,* in the GA in Amsterdam: Bicker Papers, 717 and Backer Papers, 66 respectively.

14 N. Witsen, *Moscovische Reyse* (ed. T.J.G. Locher and p. de Buck) 3 vols (The Hague 1966-7), p. 441; Parival, *op. cit.*, p. 25; and Sir William Temple, *Observations upon the United Provinces of the Netherlands*, (ed. G.N. Clark) (Cambridge 1932), p. 96.

15 E.H. Erikson, *Childhood and Society*, revised edn, (Harmondsworth 1965); the Yurok are described in ch. 4.

16 Amsterdam, GA, Curatoren van de openbare gymnasia, no. 19.

17 Joannes Backer, *Augustissimae societatis indiae orientalis encomium* (Amsterdam 1678); Joannes Trip, *Oratio metrica de civium concordiae necessitate* (Amsterdam 1681); N. Witsen, 'Kort verhael van mijn levensloop', ed. P. Scheltema in his *Aemstel's Oudheid* 6 (Amsterdam 1872), p. 41.

18 For attendance at Leyden and Franeker, see W.N. du Rieu (ed.), *Album studiosorum academiae Lugduno Batavae* (The Hague 1875); S.J. Fockema Andreae and T.J. Meijer (eds), *Album studiosorum academiae Franekerensis* (Franeker 1968).

19 For a good short account of the Athenaeum in the seventeenth century, P. Dibon, *La philosophie néerlandaise au siécle d'or* (Paris 1954), pp. 220f.

From Entrepreneur to Rentier (page 101)

1 Calculations from the *libri di nobili* of 1594 (BCV, Donà 225) and 1719, BCV, Cicogna 913).

2 E. Rodenwalt, 'Untersuchungen über die Biologie des venezianisches Adels', *Homo* 8 (1957). Rodenwalt also remarked on the fact that 40 per cent of marriages were childless or produced only one child, and explained this by the possible prevalence of gonorrhea among the nobles; but J.C. Davis, *The Decline of the Venetian Nobility as a Ruling Class* (Baltimore 1962), p. 62, notes that children who died in infancy were often not recorded in the sources Rodenwalt used.

3 H. van Dijk and D.J. Roorda, 'Sociale mobiliteit onder regenten van de Republiek', in *Tijdschrift voor Geschiedenis* (1971).

4 J.E. Elias, *De Vroedschap van Amsterdam* vol. 1 (Haarlem 1903), expresses these results in tabular form.

5 Davis, *op. cit.*, ch. 2, suggests that the rich nobles were getting richer and the poor nobles poorer.

6 This change has interested historians of both cities. On Venice, A. Stella, 'La crisi economica veneziana', *Archivio Veneto* 58 (1956); and G. Cozzi, *Il doge Nicolò Contarini* (Venice/Rome 1958), ch. 1; on Amsterdam, G.W. Kernkamp, 'Historie en Regeering', in A. Bredius (ed.), *Amsterdam in de 17e eeuw* 3 vols (The Hague 1897-), pp. 107f.; W. van Ravesteyn, *Onderzoeking over de ontwikkeling van Amsterdam* (Amsterdam 1906), p. 186; Van Dijk and Roorda, *op. cit.*

7 Carleton, quoted by Cozzi, *op. cit.*, p. 15n; *Relatione del politico governo di Venezia* (1620), anonymous, in British Museum, Add. Mss 18, 660, f. 144.

8 L. van Aitzema, *Saken van Staat en Oorlogh*, vol. 3 (The Hague 1669), p. 762.

9 The *capitano* of Padua quoted by D. Beltrami, *Forze di lavoro e proprietà fondiarià* (Venice/Rome 1961), p. 52; on the thirteenth century, G. Cracco, *Societa e stato nel medioevo veneziano* (Florence 1967), p. 82; on the ninth century, G. Luzzatto, *An Economic History of Italy*, English trans. (London 1961), p. 35.

10 H. Brugmans, 'Handel en nijverheid', in A. Bredius (ed.), *Amsterdam in de 17e eeuw* I (The Hague, 1897), p. 158; and G.J. Renier, *The Dutch Nation* (London 1944), p. 105, are well-known examples among others.

11 Of the four burgomasters in 1652, one, Nicolaes Corver,* was a merchant. As for the councillors, the following were involved in trade: J. Backer,* A. Bicker,* C. Bicker,* J. Blaeu,* S. Does,* C. Dronckelaer,* J. Huydecoper,* J. van Neck,* A. Pater,* J. van de Poll,* J. Rendorp,* G. Reynst,* S. Rijck,* W. Six,* H. Spiegel,* J. Vlooswijck* and C. Vrij. * The following were company directors: W. Backer,* R. Bicker,* C. Burgh,* S. Hoorn,* N. Pancras,* L. Reynst,* G. Valckenier,* C. Witsen.*

12 F. Seneca, *Leonardo Donà* (Padua 1959), p. 7.

13 This point emphasized by Van Dijk and Roorda, *op. cit.*

14 Table from Van Dijk and Roorda.

15 See, besides Stella, *op. cit.*, S.J. Woolf, 'Venice and the terraferma' in B. Pullan (ed.), *Crisis and change in the Venetian economy* (London 1968); D. Beltrami, *Foreze di lavoro e proprietà fondiaria* (Venice-Rome 1961), who stresses the agricultural improvements made in the period; and R. Romano, 'L'Italia nella crisi del secolo 17', *Studi Storici* (1968), who stresses the economic depression.

16 On pirates, see A. Tenenti, *Piracy and the Decline of Venice*, English trans. (London 1967). On wheat prices, M. Aymard, *Venise, Raguse et le commerce du blé* (Paris 1966), pp. 1f.

17 Beltrami (as note 15) p. 61.

18 On Zen,* see Cozzi, *op. cit.*, p. 229f; A. Colluraffi, *Il nobile veneto* (Venice 1623), p. 179: P. Sarpi (attributed), *Opinione toccante il governo della repubblica veneziana* (London 1788), p. 27; Muazzo quoted by Davis, *op. cit.*, p. 43n.

19 V. Scamozzi, *Idea dell'architettura universale* (Venice 1615), pp. 285f. Compare F. Barbieri, 'Le ville dello Scamozzi', *Bollettino Centro A. Palladio* XI (1969), which relates artistic and economic trends.

20 On 'unconscious history' see F. Braudel, 'History and the social sciences', in P. Burke (ed.), *Economy and society in early modern Europe,* (London 1972), pp. 26f.

21 A. Smith, *Wealth of Nations,* (I used the London 1904 edition), Book 3, ch. 4.

22 P.C. Hooft, *Rampsaligheden der Verheffinge van den huize van Medicis* (Amsterdam 1661), pp. 5f., 22.

23 R.P. Dore, *Education in Tokugawa Japan* (London 1965), p. 218.

24 G. Tomasi di Lampedusa, *Il Gattopardo* (Milan 1966 ed.) p. 24; on the seventeenth century as an age of economic depression, P. Chaunu, *La civilisation de l'Europe classique* (Paris 1966), part 2; E. Hobsbawm, 'The crisis of the seventeenth century', in T. Aston (ed.) *Crisis in Europe* (London 1965). On Venice in particular, D. Sella, *Commerci e industrie a Venezia nel secolo xvii* (Venice/Rome 1961); J. Addison, *Remarks on several parts of Europe* (London 1705), pp. 83f. F. Pannocchieschi made the same point about new nobles moving out of trade in his *Relazione*, edited by P. Molmenti in his *Curiosità di storia veneziana* (Bologna 1919), p. 313.

25 On the Dutch economy, see Brugmans, *op. cit.*, pp. 112f; I. Schöffer, 'Did Holland's golden age coincide with a period of crisis?', *Acta Historiae Neerlandicae* I (1966); J.A. Faber, 'The decline of the Baltic grain-trade in the second half of the seventeenth century', in the same volume of the same journal; J.G. van Dillen, *Van rijkdom en regenten* (The Hague 1970). Statistics conveniently available in H.E. Becht, *Statistisch Gegevens betreffend den Handels omzet van de Republik* (The Hague 1908).

26 One way of measuring the increase in business is to look at the growth of the minor offices in the government of Amsterdam, offices like those of the commissioners; there were 22 minor officials in 1631 but 46 in 1674, according to the lists in the *kohieren* of those years. On charisma

and the unheroic bourgeois, J. Schumpeter, *Capitalism, Socialism and Democracy* (London 1943), p. 137; I owe this last reference to Rupert Wilkinson.

27 B.H. Slicher van Bath, 'Report on the study of historical demography in the Netherlands', *Afdeling Agrarische Geschiedenis, Bijdragen* 11 (1964).

INDEX